PRAISE FOR *THE PARENT COMPASS*

"At a time when parents are bombarded with so much contradictory advice about their children's education that it's a wonder they can even breathe (let alone think), *The Parent Compass* offers counsel that is wise, calm, comprehensive, and most important of all, well-informed. These are experts you can trust."

— William Deresiewicz, *New York Times* bestselling author of *Excellent Sheep: The Miseducation of the American Elite and the Way to a Meaningful Life*

"Superbly researched with anecdotes that bring parent etiquette to life—a phrase that I just love! Fair warning, expect to have your hand metaphorically 'slapped' now and again, as it is a necessary part of learning how to best support our teens. Fortunately, this is done in kindness with the insights of how to do better for the overall well-being of your teenager. Follow their advice and you will have a healthy teenager; better yet, ten years from now, you'll have a healthy and contributing young adult."

— Dr. Mike Riera, author of *Staying Connected to Your Teenager* and head of school, Brentwood School

"*The Parent Compass* helps parents resist the urge to hover and micromanage, and guides them to reflect deeply on their actions and make important changes to support their teen's long-term well-being and success."

— Dr. Denise Pope, senior lecturer, Stanford University and co-founder, Challenge Success

"This is the book that every parent needs. *The Parent Compass* helps us understand how to appropriately engage with our teens and how to

parent with more awareness. The pages are brimming with powerful advice about navigating the parenting waters."

    —Tiffany Shlain, author of *24/6: The Power of Unplugging One Day a Week* and Emmy-nominated filmmaker

"At a time when our love for our children is being contorted into actions we may no longer recognize as parents, this book offers a compassionate but firm user's manual for how to navigate some of the most treacherous years of a young person's life. Parenting is the most difficult role in society today, bar none: the sense of scarcity and abundance of fear have turned us upside down in many ways. *The Parent Compass* is the guide that will help us to stop snatching defeat from the jaws of victory and bring us back to principles. And when the principles are clear, the decisions are easy."

    —Than Healy, head of school, Menlo School

"It's hard enough for today's teens to feel constant pressure from the outside world to knock it out of the park further than everyone else around them, but when parents overstep boundaries by writing their kid's papers, speaking for them, and micromanaging their lives into the ground, that's crossing a line. *The Parent Compass* is a truly necessary resource that helps keep parents in check when the urge strikes to helicopter and bulldoze and interfere in the parts of our teenage kid's lives that should be up to them to manage."

    —Lisa Sugarman, nationally syndicated columnist, radio show host, speaker, and author of *How to Raise Perfectly Imperfect Kids— And Be OK with It*

"Parenting teenagers is hard work, plain and simple. In an era where common sense seems to have disappeared and our parental anxieties rule the day, *The Parent Compass* is just what families need to help guide them through the forest of adolescence. *The Parent Compass* is an excellent tool to reassure parents to trust their instincts and ignore the drop-off line gossip and cocktail party hysteria. The advice it provides will allow all of us to more thoughtfully and lovingly parent our children while still preparing them to be healthy adults who can make it in the world."

    —Chris Mazzola, head of school, The Branson School

"This really is a remarkable book. It strikes a balance between being an involved parent and being a helicopter parent, between a clear-on-the-sidelines parent and everything in the trenches; it saves the day."

    —Brian Rogers, faculty, Webb Schools, and author of *The Whole of the Moon*

"This is a very timely and important book . . . for parents . . . [and] the landscape is ever changing. *The Parent Compass* provides great advice and guidance from experts of all types."

    —Michael Dennin, professor of physics and astronomy and Vice Provost for Teaching and Learning, UC–Irvine

"Finally—a book that calls out what we know to be true about how overly involved parents can negatively impact a child's development, while offering simple ways to implement practical advice on how to help our children thrive during their teenage years. A must read for any parent who wants an emotionally healthy, confident, independent child!"

    —Jill Quigley, principal, middle and upper schools, TVT Community Day School

"This book offers a refreshing look at current foibles of all involved in the educational process and provides common sense suggestions for better parenting."

    —Linda Winrow, high school teacher and educator for nearly fifty years

THE
PARENT
COMPASS

FAMILIUS

Published by Familius LLC, www.familius.com
1254 Commerce Way, Sanger, CA 93657

Familius books are available at special discounts for bulk purchases,
whether for sales promotions or for family or corporate use.
For more information, contact Familius Sales at 559-876-2170
or email orders@familius.com.

Some names have been changed to protect the privacy
of the parents and students discussed.

Library of Congress Control Number: 2020941630

Print ISBN 978-1-64170-288-1
Ebook ISBN 978-1-64170-436-6

Printed in the United States of America

Edited by Kaylee Mason and Alison Strobel
Cover and book design by Mara Harris

10 9 8 7 6 5 4 3 2 1

First Edition

THE
PARENT
COMPASS

NAVIGATING YOUR TEEN'S
WELLNESS & ACADEMIC JOURNEY
IN TODAY'S COMPETITIVE WORLD

Cynthia Clumeck Muchnick, MA &
Jenn Curtis, MSW

DEDICATION

To Justin, Jacob, Ross, and Alexa, who complete my world, teach me life lessons, and help remind me to follow my parent compass every single day.

And to Adam, my cheerleader and best friend in all that I do, who has partnered and parented with me through every high and low for the past twenty-five-plus years.

I love you all.

—Cindy Clumeck Muchnick

To Zoe and Corinne, who make me strive to be the mama they believe I am and who daily push me to tackle my goals.

And to Mike, who patiently navigates the parenting maze with me and for whose unfailing encouragement and selflessness I am forever grateful.

—Jenn Curtis

CONTENTS

FOREWORD

In order to write my dissertation on student engagement with learning, I spent a year shadowing five high-achieving high school students in Silicon Valley. Unfortunately, I didn't find the kind of engagement I was hoping to document. Instead of being genuinely motivated and excited by their courses and activities, many of the students admitted to "doing school"—going through the motions, cheating, cutting corners, and ultimately not learning the material in depth. Most felt overloaded by homework, exams, and extracurricular activities that interfered with their sleep and social lives. The pressure to over-achieve eventually took its toll on them and led to high levels of physical and emotional distress and exhaustion.

A few years later, I co-founded Challenge Success, an organization that promotes student well-being and academic engagement. Our surveys of over 200,000 high school students from high-performing schools showed similar results: students were stressed, exhausted, and disengaged from school. Our findings are underscored by recent reports that have classified students from high-achieving communities as an "at-risk" population— along with young people living in poverty, foster care, and those with incarcerated parents.[1] While some stress is necessary and can be healthy for adolescent development, we know that an undue amount of pressure placed on kids at home or school can be harmful to their well-being.

As parents, we all want our kids to master certain skills and concepts, but our largely singular focus on a narrow notion of success as defined by grades, test scores, and college admission has resulted in a lack of attention to other components of a successful life—the ability to experience joy and good health; to make ethical decisions; and to be independent, resilient, and engaged critical thinkers. Overzealous parents tend to check grade reports daily, edit essays, correct problem sets, and hire tutors and consultants—all in the name of academic achievement. But in doing so, they often lose sight of the bigger picture. Many well-meaning parents give their teens a pass from doing chores so that they can have more time to study, allow teens to be on phones and devices at the dinner table and late into the night, intervene with teachers and coaches instead of letting students advocate for themselves, and hover and helicopter without realizing that they are actually impeding important growth and maturation.

So you can imagine my excitement when I heard about plans for *The Parent Compass: Navigating Your Teen's Wellness & Academic Journey in Today's Competitive World*. The book offers practical tips and tools for parents who want to raise healthy, resilient, and motivated adults. This is something we all want for our tweens and teens, but in our hyper-competitive culture, this is not an easy task. Cynthia and Jenn have been working with teens for a combined thirty-plus years and have their fingers on the pulse of the ever-changing adolescent landscape. They have created a much-needed compass to help parents resist the urge to micromanage and to help each of us reflect deeply on our actions and make changes to support our children's long-term well-being and success. I hope you will spend time with this book, completing the exercises and questionnaires, reading through the scenarios, discussing sections with your family, and helping to spread these ideas to others by modeling positive parenting in your community. Let *The Parent Compass* be your guide to better parenting.

Denise Pope, PhD, is a Senior Lecturer at Stanford University and the co-founder of Challenge Success, a nonprofit that partners with schools, families, and communities to support student well-being and engagement with learning.

INTRODUCTION

"Adolescence is a period of rapid changes. Between the ages of thirteen and seventeen, a parent can age as much as twenty years." —Anonymous

Parents, have you ever asked yourself, "What am I doing wrong?" Or maybe you've wondered, "How can I better support my teen?" In our combined thirty years as educational consultants, speakers, and mothers of a total of six children, we have often heard these questions. The parents asking them are eagerly searching for wisdom and tools as they agonize over helping their over-stressed, over-programmed, and over-exhausted kids both succeed and be happy during their tween and teenage years.

In recent years, the parenting world has been rocked by the high-profile cases of "Operation Varsity Blues," the college admission scandal that uncovered an unsettling trend of paranoid parents resorting to fraud and bribery to help their kids get into college. And these shocking stories of parental overreach have come during an era in which external stressors on our children are at a record high: a 2017 study found that 3.2 million teens, or 13.3 percent of the teenage population, had experienced a major depressive episode during the previous year.[1] Add to all of that the immense social precarity, economic uncertainty, and academic anxiety brought on by the epochal COVID-19 pandemic, and it becomes clear that now, when we are all grasping at straws for some sense of hope and assurance, is the time for a book that can help parents parent. Now, more than ever, is the time to help parents figure out how to behave appropriately while safely, supportively, and successfully guiding their tweens and teens through the maze of middle and high school—and especially through the college admission process.

But let us be clear: the book you hold in your hands is intentionally not a book rife with tips on "how to get your child into college." Rather, it is a framework for how you as a parent can better support and communicate with your children, no matter what is going on in the world around you. We can all agree that, in general, we want the same things for our children. We want them to grow into kind, happy, healthy people who possess a desire to contribute to our planet and to find a career that brings them joy. We can also agree that our intention isn't to raise bullies or apathetic, listless human beings. But the question is, as parents, how exactly do we achieve these goals?

In our professional roles, we have seen the insane lengths that some of today's parents are willing to go to just to help their kids get into college; it has become clear that despite our common goals, our generation of parents has gotten way off track. We are angry with the behavior of many parents of teens and with the pressure put on these teens during the college admission process, so—after witnessing firsthand what that pressure has done to parents and students alike—we were compelled to write this book. It was born out of deep feelings of sadness for our overly stressed-out students and our desire to put things right and to help teens come out of these difficult years happy, productive, and intact—not frazzled, depressed, and burned out.

We have seen parents who talk for their children and kids who have no opinions, parents who are inflexible and kids who shy away from them, parents who get too caught up in the name-brand schools and kids who are unable to find the best fit. We have seen all too intimately the consequences when parents behave swell-headedly, believing in and even bragging about the status that comes when their child attends a highly ranked school and appearing embarrassed or disappointed when their child attends a less well-known school. We have seen too many parents who can't manage to get out of the way long enough to let their children experience where their interests can lead them. We have seen so much of the bad.

But we have also seen so much of the good. Over the years, we have keenly watched those students who soar and their parents who patiently watch them do so. We have observed the parenting etiquette that leads to happy, successful, and balanced teens. We have seen parents who trust and kids who reciprocate, parents who respect and kids who likewise respect, parents who are present and who take the time to get to know their children—and in turn kids who feel valued and have the room to achieve their wildest dreams. This is why we wrote this book. *The Parent Compass* is a call to action and a reference guide that provides tools for better navigation and parenting etiquette. With *The Parent Compass* as a resource, parents can learn to adopt a proper, appropriate etiquette that leads to their child's academic success and emotional well-being.

But before we jump in, we feel compelled to offer three critical author notes. First, through the process of writing this book, we found ourselves straddling a fine line. Our primary goal is to provide content and anecdotes to calm the frightening frenzy that has consumed so many families; we aim to help parents allow their teens to own the process of discovering who they are, navigating school academically and socially, and making mistakes along the way. In researching and writing to that end, though, we experienced an equal pull to share practical background information as it pertains to academics and, more specifically, the college admission process. Our intention is not to fan the flames of middle- and high-school parent panic; instead, we feel that it is important to offer valuable resources, terminology, and definitions in order to better educate parents and ensure that they have a more complete picture of middle- and high-school life today. Armed with this foundational information, you as parents will be better equipped—and as a result more comfortable—to assume a "hands off" role in your child's process.

Second, for the purposes of keeping this book simple, we use the traditional pronouns "him" and "her" when referring to teens and alternate back and forth between them. We refer to parents (our reading audience) as "parents" and "you." (That said, we recognize that this book will be read by people of diverse genders and family configurations. Rest assured that, while writing these chapters, we had you in mind as well.) And, when we, your co-authors, refer to ourselves and speak to you, we use both the collective "I" and "we"; but please know that we are both speaking to you and sharing our agreed upon philosophy with you, our readers.

And, third, readers, we are on this journey with you. We are not perfect parents, either. Admittedly, in our personal parent navigation, we, too, have strayed from the path, bumping into walls in our own parenting mazes. We have made—and continue to make—mistakes along the way, and so we continue to modify our own parenting choices, grow, self-correct, and try harder to practice the parent compass lessons we share in the following pages.

Our goal is to help parents better understand their appropriate position in their kids' middle and high school years, ultimately culminating in the college admission process. This is a role that doesn't cross inappropriate, blurry lines; it models, cheers, and trusts as opposed to forces, coddles, and controls. The tools presented in *The Parent Compass* come from our own community observations and from our personal experiences as parents as well as from situations we have witnessed with our student clients or between our students and their parents. The ideas we share also come from our hours of interviews with educational leaders, teachers, and counselors who have boots on the ground in today's middle and high schools; authors who are also researching our teen population; and experts in teen psychology whose insights and research bolster our parent compass plan.

As this book's opening quote warns, during their child's adolescent years, "parents can age as much as twenty years." We understand that this is a trying time. Indeed, it is a downright uncertain time, and it is a time that looks different for every family based not only on what is going on in the world of college admission but also what is playing out in the world at large. We know students well: we have counseled them and consoled them, and we are here to give you the answers you need to relate to your teen in a more healthy, productive, and beneficial way. Let *The Parent Compass: Navigating Your Teen's Wellness & Academic Journey in Today's Competitive World* be your reference guide and resource. It can show you how you, too, can make it through those tween and teen years and keep your relationship with your children intact, even helping them find their next stage of happiness, self-reliance, and purpose in their life's journey to college and beyond.

—Cynthia Clumeck Muchnick and Jenn Curtis

CHAPTER 1:
HOW TO USE YOUR PARENT COMPASS

In a recent consultation with a student and her mother, I attempted to gather information from the seventeen-year-old young woman sitting in front of me. Nearly ten minutes into the meeting, though, I noted that the student had yet to speak; her eyes were downcast while her mother blathered on, often comparing the student to her older sister. Attempting to loop the young woman into the conversation, I asked her what sorts of things interested her. She stared at me blankly, clearly at a loss for words. Her face scrunched up in pain as she squirmed on the couch, frantically glancing back and forth from me to her mother. Eventually, she turned to her mom in exasperation, pleading only, "Mom!" while she further contorted her face—still unable to answer my question. I was floored.

This student had never spoken for herself.

We've all witnessed the out of control parent screeching from the sports sidelines, carelessly embarrassing himself and his horrified child. We've all looked on while a parent dismissively answers a question intended for her capable teenage child or takes the helm on a final project so that her child doesn't perform poorly on it. We've all known the parent who wants to make himself heard by teachers and administrators but who somehow can't recognize when he has simply gone too far. And we've all noticed the parent who posts bragging comments on social media detailing her teen's every accomplishment, whether big or small. And then we've all experienced the nuances: the parent who completes her son's homework assignment over breakfast (but of course her son was "dictating the answers") and the one who completes some sections on college applications (but of course his daughter was "sitting nearby"). Maybe that parent is actually you. Or maybe you are trying not to be that parent but are nevertheless beginning to feel the strain in your relationship with your child as the pressure of academics builds.

The role of a parent is complicated and tricky. Navigating that role with confidence, trust, and patience is no easy task, and it is full of twists and turns—an intricate parenting maze that fundamentally necessitates constant self-evaluation. *But at its very core, following your parent compass demands that you take the time to truly know yourself and your child.* The concept of a parent compass was gleaned from years of closely studying parents who fostered their kids' success, and simultaneously watching from the sidelines those parents who hindered it. *The Parent Compass* is a collection of stories, suggestions, and ideas that deal with how to behave as a parent in a world full of intense academic and social competition. This book also infuses current research and statistics, news articles, and insight from scores of interviews with experts in the psychology and education fields as well as wisdom gleaned from teachers, headmasters, counselors, and other professionals who work with today's tweens and teens day in and day out. We discuss appropriate behaviors within the context of your relationship with your growing children—those behaviors that promote a respectful relationship with a well-adjusted, healthy, productive student rather than a strained relationship with an unhappy, insecure, exasperated one. Following your parent compass involves being aware of your child's behaviors and interactions with other adults, including teachers, coaches, and administrators.

It is hard for parents to practice what they know is right when everyone around them seems to be frantically tutoring, managing, and helicoptering. While well intentioned, many parents don't know how best to support their children during this sensitive and stressful time. Indeed, it is common for us to encounter overbearing parents who mean well but who ultimately render their kids helpless, unfulfilled, and without a voice—and push their kids away in the process. In his work, author Mike Riera aptly discusses the transition in a parent's role from manager to colleague and consultant. As students transition from middle to high school, at some point, they "fire" their parents as managers; this is a sign of independence. As painful as this may feel to parents, it is better not to fight back but instead to grieve a little and then hope to be hired back as "consultants."[1] We agree with this analysis, and most importantly, we think that parents need to remember to be cheerleaders for their kids and to help them find and pursue their interests—both in the classroom and out of it—whatever they may be.

The parent compass is a *movement.* It is a call to action—to check yourself, to check your fellow parents, to take an honest look at why you behave the way you do when it comes to your child's academics, and to make changes so that today's tween and teen generation can learn grit and resilience and can contribute meaningfully in their gifted or even not-so-gifted areas. The goal of checking your compass is to help you modify your behavior and, in turn, your mindset. It is an antidote to over-parenting. It is to help you parent with intention. It is to hold you accountable so that you do not fall prey to parenting peer pressure, college rankings, and media hype about colleges. We believe that kids respond best to parents who inherently trust them—in their day-to-day activities and also in their decision-making skills—and we extend that principle to what feels right for the college process.

One high school headmaster eloquently summarized so much of what *The Parent Compass* is trying to teach parents.

> Families, too, play a role in empowering students. We need you to show your belief in them. It's tempting in this day and age to step in: to take control when you see your child struggling, to solve the problem for them. But this sends the message, "I don't believe you can do this. I don't believe that you're capable of handling this yourself." That's not what you mean, but that's what a sixteen year old will hear. Here, too, we can take the long view—we want them to learn to advocate for themselves. Your calming influence is what will empower them to get there.[2]

Parents, as you begin to embrace the intentional parenting strategies suggested in the following pages, also ask yourself, what is the end result that you want with your relationship with your teen? Picture yourself ten, twenty, even thirty years from now. Is what you are doing *now* paving the way for the relationship you want *then*?

Don't Be a Helicopter, Snowplow, or Tiger Parent

Hovering, micromanaging, and making a lot of unnecessary noise in your child's upbringing only adds stress and worry to an already overly busy time. If this describes you, we're sorry to break the news: *you are a helicopter parent.* If you are constantly meddling and stepping in to clear the way of every obstacle for your child—to groom the path, so to speak—then, well, we're sorry to break the news: *you are also a snowplow parent.* If you are strict, demanding, inflexible, and maybe even milita-ristic with hard rules for your kids, *you are also a tiger parent.* And, if you can answer yes to any of the following questions, you are not effectively navigating with the parent compass:

- Do you contact your child's high school teachers or administra-tors instead of allowing your child to self-advocate?

- Do you complain to your teen's coach about playing time?

- Do you hover over your child when he is doing homework or studying for a test, or do you get overly involved in helping with or overseeing his schoolwork? (Flashback: were you the parent at the playground who habitually hovered over your child to protect him from falling?)

- Do you wake up your teen every day for school?

- Have you ever woken up your child during the night to study more? (Yes, we have heard of this shocking parent behavior, too!)

- Do you deliver a book or homework assignment to school every time that your teen forgets hers? Or maybe it's her lunch, coat, or a forgotten item for her extracurricular activity?

- Do you try to ensure that your child has a certain teacher for his classes or coach for his teams?

- Do you select your teen's activities or push her toward certain ones?

- Do you try to pave the way for your child to be academically successful? Or do you intervene so that he has more opportunity in his extracurricular activities?

- Do you have strong opinions about who your teen's friends are?

- Do you make hard, or perhaps extreme, rules such as very early curfews and impossible homework expectations—and unreasonable punishments for not adhering to these rules? Would you describe you or your spouse's style as military style?

- Do you hire extra tutors in multiple subjects to help your teen with homework?

Unfortunately helicopter, snowplow, and tiger parents do not practice parenting etiquette and are creating a generation known as snowflakes (or teacups): college students who are fragile because they have no experience with adversity or failure and are ill-equipped to deal with even the most mundane of tasks, like waking themselves up for class or self-advocating with a professor or teaching assistant. But there is hope for even the biggest helicopter parent! We intend to help struggling parents understand more about how their behaviors could be negatively impacting the relationship with their teen and, what's more, could be rendering their teen helpless and hopeless. And we intend to offer strategies to help fix and improve these relationships.

On the other hand, if you answer yes to these, you are likely following your parent compass:

- Do you allow your child to fail or falter in school?

- Do you praise effort more than outcome and talk through lessons learned?

- Do you support your teen's interests even if they differ from your own?

- Do you urge your teen to seek teachers' feedback whenever he is struggling with a class or when he doesn't understand a concept?

- Do you have your teen contribute financially (e.g., pay for her own gas) or do household chores and tasks (e.g., make her bed, set or clear the table, or do dishes)?

- Do you encourage your teen to self-advocate (speak first to a teacher or coach if he has a problem or issue)?

- Do you encourage your child to respectfully speak up when she has an opposing opinion?

While this second list of questions may be hard to discipline yourself to practice, fostering autonomy in your home will afford your teen a large payoff later: he will be better equipped for life outside your home in school, college, and the real world beyond. Taking a long-view approach in parenting—imagining your child as an adult and over a twenty-year timespan—instead of obsessing over every small infraction, decision, or mistake he makes, will yield better long-term results in your child's social and emotional development. *If you invest your time in embracing and practicing parent compass strategies, you will raise a well-adjusted and happy adult.* Consider this parent's summation: "This is a great accountability question for parents. When you find yourself intruding in your teen's life, ask yourself if helping them the way you feel is most natural is really going to help them down the road? Is helping them actually hurting them? Does your help disable them from learning hard lessons they'll thank you for later? . . . I often use this phrase: the further out I can see into the future, the better the decision I make today for my child."[3]

"Learning to cope with manageable threats (like failing a test or forgetting one's lines in a play) to our physical and social well-being is critical for the development of resilience."[4]

Your Teen's Developmental Stage

Let's take a minute to look at what your child is experiencing developmentally between the ages of twelve and eighteen and how that impacts your parenting behavior. For those precious six years, she is testing, exploring, trying on, embracing, and rejecting in order to determine what her role in society looks like. Who is she? What career will she pursue? What are her values? These are questions that she is naturally and developmentally asking herself. Furthermore, let's consider your child's brain. Scientists tell us that the human brain is not fully developed until the age of twenty-five. Yes, twenty-five! Guess what? Your child will have already graduated from college and entered the workforce at that point. So these critical years are defined by intense self-discovery, making mistakes, and learning from them. At its very core, this stage necessitates trying on individuation from mom and dad.

It follows, then, that an overreaching parent will impair a child's ability to successfully navigate this crucial developmental stage. Overscheduling, rigidity, speaking for a child, pressure to hold certain opinions, and inflexibility on the part of a parent will impede his ability to authentically explore the world around him. Parents who pigeonhole their child into a certain vision that *they* have for him, or who don't allow him the freedom to try things on, are significantly impairing their child's ability to navigate this stage successfully. And what happens when a child cannot successfully navigate this stage? Well, naturally, he will have no clue how to determine how he fits into the world. (Remember our main character in the opening paragraph?)

Signs of a Happy Teenager

How do you know if your teen is actually happy? While this age is often hormonal, volatile, and difficult to decipher, it is also a time of joy and immense growth and exploration. Electronic devices might get in the way of your ability to best evaluate your teen in terms of her happiness quotient, but in general you might find a happy kid to be someone who generally seems to be balancing the rigor of school with the emotions of friendships and romantic relationships, and who seems to be eating well and getting enough sleep. Happy teens have interests or hobbies that they enjoy pursuing. Of course they won't always have a smile on their faces—which may hint at the thoughts swirling inside, so parents, don't be afraid to ask them. We offer many questions to get conversations moving later in this chapter.

In a recent Pew Research Survey of thirteen- to seventeen-year-olds across the country, 70 percent of those surveyed cited anxiety and depression as a major concern. In fact, that measure placed the highest, above any other concern, including bullying, drug abuse, and teen pregnancy.[5] You know your child best, and if your instinct tells you that things seem to be off, then listen to it. Common signs to watch for could be a drop in grades, apathy, weight gain or weight loss, a withdrawn nature when they are typically not withdrawn, tearfulness, or severe mood swings, among other behaviors.

Communicating Well with Your Teen

Ask the Right Questions

Do you sometimes find your teen answering you in one-word answers—"fine," "good," "sure,"—or, worse, in grunts, eye rolls, or shoulder shrugs when you ask a question? Are conversations becoming shorter, less enthusiastic, or few and far between? Are there even tears sometimes when you ask non-threatening questions? Asking the right questions elicits productive dialogue and also empowers your high school teen. How many of you ask the question, "How was school today?" or, "How did you do on your test today?" when your child slides into the car or shuffles through the door after school? Why not ask better questions that draw out more meaningful content and require more thoughtful responses?

Here are some questions to ask your kids at the end of the school day that necessitate thoughtful responses:[6]

- If I called your teacher tonight, what would s/he tell me about you?

- How did you help somebody today?

- Can you tell me one thing you learned today?

- When were you the happiest today?

- When were you bored today?

- What would you change about school lunch?

- What was one thing you read/learned at school today?

- Who did you sit with at lunch today, and what did you laugh about?

- What was something good that happened today?

- If today had a theme song, what would it be?

- Which class is your easiest and which is your hardest?

- Which teacher do you like the best and why? And the least?

- If you were a teacher what class would you teach?

Additionally, author and "question expert" Warren Berger has written several books on the power and art of asking good questions. Below are a few of his suggested questions to encourage more meaningful conversations with teens. You can try to answer these questions yourself, too, so that you and your teen can share your thoughts with each other:[7]

- What was the most difficult problem you had today? How could you have handled this differently?

- What have you failed at this week?

- If you were an inventor—what would you invent, and why?

- What was your first thought when you woke up today?

- Who in your class seems lonely?

- What do you think is the biggest challenge facing our world today?

- What do you struggle with on a day-to-day basis?

- What have you always wanted to try?

- If you could start your own nonprofit, what would it be?

- What would be the title of your autobiography?

- If you had to live in another country for a year, where would that be?

- What is your biggest dream in life?

- When you have failed, how did you respond?

- If people were asked how you treat them, what do you think they'd say?

- What is your sentence? (Meaning, if you had to summarize your life in one sentence, what would that sentence be?)

- What is your tennis ball? (What is the thing that you chase as intently as a dog chases a tennis ball?)

- What are you trying to get better at?

In Kelly Corrigan's *New York Times*–bestselling book *Tell Me More: Stories about the 12 Hardest Things I'm Learning to Say*, the author explores the statements that we need to share in order to have more meaningful relationships. The most important that she explores for the context of this book is the phrase "Tell me more," which is simply a head nod and an "uh huh," encouraging your teen to share more and letting him know that you hear him, you see him, and you are intently listening and want more. (This is *not* the same "uh huh" you might offer as your eyes are fixated on your phone while you scroll through the day's text messages. More on that in Chapter 6.)

Finally, the parent compass movement wholly resonates with this quote from Nobel laureate scientist Isidor Isaac "Izzy" Rabi, as he reflects on his mother's line of questioning when he was a child: "My mother made me a scientist without ever intending to. Every other Jewish mother in Brooklyn would ask her child after school, 'So? Did you learn anything today?' But not my mother. 'Izzy,' she would say, 'did you ask a good question today?' That difference—asking good questions—made me become a scientist."[8]

Become a Better Listener

Hearing is one thing, but *listening* is quite another. Hearing allows words and sounds to be perceived by one's ears; it's a passive action. But listening—listening requires work, practice, and concentration, which require active participation in an exchange. Practice presence. *Be* present. Focus on your child. Hear every. single. word. Look her in the eye and absorb what she is saying. It may help to picture it this way: if you have a career outside of the home, you are familiar with those situations when you attend a board meeting or sit down with a boss, colleague, or superior. You must be on your best behavior and offer all of your attention. Parents, extend the same courtesy to your own kid. There are hundreds of articles written on the topic of listening, and a simple Internet search will yield them. We encourage you to read a few. Whether you have an open, communicative teen or a reserved, less conversant teen, when your teen does open up to you, be prepared for floodgates to open. Often, you are the safest audience for your teen to vent to, unload on, and share private stories and situations. Understand that these confessions are not necessarily for you to solve or fix; mostly your child needs someone to listen and receive this information that may have been bottled up for a day, a week, or even a month (more on refraining from fixing in Chapter 3).

About Beth: A Parent's Perspective

When Sarah's daughter, Beth, started attending boarding school across the country, Sarah received a weekly phone call from her daughter. These calls were often full of dramatic and heavy news, whether social, academic, or athletic. Because of this, they were difficult for Sarah to receive, as she was not geographically nearby to offer a hug or direct eye contact or observe her daughter's body language. After sometimes thirty minutes of unloading, Beth hung up the phone and Sarah (and often her husband) was left with the fallout of this conversation—and they panicked. Should they get on a plane and fly there to help? Should they alert Beth's dorm advisor or a teacher to check on Beth's mental state? Sarah and her husband lost nights of sleep, tossing and turning as they considered how to intervene. When they did choose to call an adult who could have eyes on their daughter, they were usually told, "I just saw her at lunch today laughing and smiling with her friends. I will keep an eye out, but everything here looks normal."

So, what were Sarah and her husband to do? Accept that they were the receptacle of a flurry of stress their daughter had been holding onto as she waited for someone she trusted to tell? But as Sarah and her husband settled into their new role, they realized that *they were her people*; now that Beth was away, she needed them to be her safety valve. *Sometimes just listening and not acting or trying to solve all problems is enough.* (This story applies to college-age teens as well. A similar pattern often occurs when kids are living on their own for the first time. Approach it the same way.)

Here are some of our listening suggestions to help get you started:

- Stop what you are doing and offer eye contact—even touch your teen's arm or hand while she speaks to you.

- Practice good posture, leaning in while spoken to. Don't cross your arms, check your phone, or be distracted by the eighteen things on your to-do list—they are patiently awaiting your attention.

- Maintain eye contact. Don't let your eyes wander all over the place.

- Use confirmation expressions, like "Mmm hmmm," while nodding your head in agreement to demonstrate that you are connecting. "Tell me more," a phrase recently re-coined by author Kelly Corrigan, can be used to encourage your teen to keep his words flowing and your ears listening.

- Parrot back or paraphrase some of the things she is telling you. This will help your teen feel authentically heard.

- Silence is okay. Sometimes a pause allows your teen to better formulate his thoughts and words. Don't feel the urge to finish his sentences or choose his words for him.

- Resist the urge to fix and problem-solve. Sometimes all your teen needs is the space to talk to someone she trusts and de-escalate the situation. Often just speaking the words to someone with whom she feels safe is enough to diffuse and lighten her load. Just listen.

- Pick a good time and location. Don't be afraid to have chats while lying on your teen's bed, enjoying a snack or meal with him in the kitchen, or hanging out on the family couch. Sometimes a casual, comfortable setting yields the best exchanges. Both of our families have puzzle tables where in-progress puzzles are always on display. Those locations can facilitate some great conversations between you and your teen.

What Happens If You Don't Follow Your Compass?

There exists mounting evidence that our children suffer when we do not follow the parent compass. In *The Price of Privilege*, psychologist Madeline Levine warns of a new at-risk group of young people: "Researchers . . . have found that America has a new group of 'at-risk' kids," she writes, "or, more accurately, a previously unrecognized and unstudied group of at-risk kids. They defy the stereotypes commonly associated with the term 'at-risk.' They are not inner-city kids growing up in harsh and unforgiving circumstances. They do not have empty refrigerators in their kitchens, roaches in their homes, metal detectors in their schools, or killings in their neighborhoods. America's newly identified at-risk group is preteens and teens from affluent, well-educated families."[9]

At best, your child might look like the child we met at the beginning of this chapter: unable to carry on a conversation with other adults, unable to identify her own likes and dislikes, unable to articulate who she is. And we'd ask you, where is the spice of life in that? But at worst, your child could develop some serious symptoms and diagnoses, most notably severe anxiety and depression, and your relationship with her could greatly suffer. Says Kirk Carapezza, for WGBH News, "The early intensity in upscale suburban families about their children's future achievement is said to be one factor behind the mental health crisis that colleges are facing. Over the past ten years, the rate of anxiety and depression among college-age students has doubled, according to researchers at the University of Michigan. Psychologists say the pressures driving these problems start long before kids set foot on campus."[10]

Parents, we implore you to take seriously what you are reading. Try the tips we offer in the ensuing pages. Some will work for you, and some will not. Perfect parents don't exist and neither do perfect teens. Spoiler alert: you will fail. And then you'll try again until you get it right—just as you're teaching your kids to do. And then you may even fail again. And again. And then get it right again. *After all, the simple fact that you are reading this book demonstrates that you want to do better. And what is wrong with attempting self-improvement? Nothing.*

Basic Parent Compass Dos and Don'ts

- Do expose, identify, facilitate, and fuel your kids' passions (and be supportive and enthusiastic if they are different from your own!).

- Do avoid advice from other parents who make you feel guilt and peer pressured in comparison to what their kids are doing.

- Do be flexible to new ideas in education, alternative routes students can take after high school, rule bending, and reinterpreting what you can do as a parent today.

- Do be an active listener.

- Don't compare your kids to other people's or friends' kids. Your kids may share classes, teams, or interests, but no two kids are the same. Allow each teen to be an individual.

- Don't be a helicopter parent who hinders your kids' expressions of their natural talents. The majority of kids do not know what they want to do with the rest of their lives, and the thought of determining it at the developmentally inappropriate age of fourteen can be paralyzing to them.

- Don't push to have it all figured out for your kids. Let them learn things in their own time and try on many passions; some preferred ones will eventually emerge.

- Don't blame yourself if your budget cannot afford extra summer programs or fancy camps or if you don't have personal connections for your teen to obtain coveted internships. Most of those supplemental activities and connections can be found for a fraction of the cost through local recreation centers, church or religious groups, community college, or college campuses.

- Don't compare your own kids to one another. Birth order, gender, your parenting experience, and plain old DNA make no two kids alike.

CHAPTER 2:
TAKE A TRIP DOWN MEMORY LANE

We feel it only appropriate to offer a fair warning at the very outset of this chapter: it's about to get real. And we mean real in the sense that we are going to ask you to do some real, honest reflection. We're going to challenge you to consider your biases, push you to think about the life experiences that influence your parenting behaviors, and nudge you toward initiating meaningful conversations with your kids. We're going to ask you about your past, help you to reflect on your present, and implore you to consider what your future will look like. In short, we are going to encourage you to be brave; to have the courage necessary to take a cold, hard look at who you are and how you behave; and to reconcile all of this before you try to lead your child through the daunting teenage years. (And if you happen to be reading this book deeper into your high school child-rearing years, that is okay, too. Parent compass concepts can be implemented at any point in your tween and teen parenting journey to guide you in new directions and teach you new tools.)

In fleshing out what we believed the parent compass to be, we had many conversations about what we felt it meant to be a kid. Naturally, we reminisced about our own experiences. We conjured up memories of riding bikes after school and gliding to the park on roller skates. We remembered parents picking up the (landline) phone receivers to implore us to "hang up and get to bed." Cell phones had yet to make an appearance, and personal computers were a whole lot clunkier and slower than they are today. Both of us relished in the memories of selecting fresh new school supplies every September (the education field clearly had a calling for us), and we agreed that while homework existed and was sometimes "hard and boring," it didn't take so long that we couldn't have family dinner and participate in after-school sports teams or dance class. There were big projects that required time immersed in library books, digging through old-fashioned card catalogs and the Dewey decimal system. One of us recalled posting "lost dog" signs on telephone poles when a friend's pet went missing. One remembered having time to be in the school musical *and* do a sport—many sports actually and not just one throughout the year—and making posters with glitter and glue for student elections. We both remembered fun summer jobs, and both of us had memories like taking trips to the local pool where there was a climb-up water slide (that was more like a ladder with a ramp attached). Weekends were, for the most part, set aside for maybe one sports game, a sleepover with a friend, and enough down-time to be ready for the week ahead. Life seemed simpler then.

Know Yourself First

Parents, the first step in navigating forward with your parent compass is, in fact, to look backward. What contributed to who you are today? To begin, take some time to think back to your own middle and high school experience. Chances are, attending school and spending free time was different for you then. You'll probably admit that you were much less programmed with sports, extracurricular activities, and long late nights of homework than your kids are, and that you spontaneously participated in more fun after-school activities: riding bikes, reading a book for pleasure, enjoy-ing a Slurpee, or ambling around the mall.

Consider where you attended middle and high school. Was it your neighborhood public school? Maybe a private school, parochial school, or boarding school? How were academics treated in your household when you were growing up? Did your parents push you to achieve? Maybe they were busy working and didn't ask you much about your classes, or perhaps school wasn't a priority in your home? Then factor in what you can recall of the kind of student you were in middle and high school. Did school come easy to you? Maybe it didn't. Did you walk, bike, or drive to school once you were of age? What activities did you do? What classes came easier to you and harder to you? Were you the oldest or the family leader of your siblings, or were you more dependent on older siblings? Were you coddled, or were you independent? Then consider your college application process (if you went to college): there were a couple of essays that you wrote by hand or, if you were lucky, on a typewriter; you applied to only a few schools; and thick or thin college decision envelopes arrived in the mailbox to deliver the news. Many, if not all, of us agree that if we were to apply to those same colleges today, we would not have a remote chance of getting in. That is quite a sad commentary on the higher stakes now in the college admission process and how laborious and stressful it has become.

We encourage you to take some time to list your reflections. Dust off the cobwebs and take a good look at who you were back then. Peruse old yearbooks or reminisce with friends. Assess yourself—consider your background, your biases, your unique experiences, *your baggage*. Now think about your personality and your values. Maybe you grew up in a home in which it was difficult to garner your dad's attention, and he only gave it to you when you achieved or won something. Naturally, you might have sought achievement after achievement just to get him to look your way, and so this impacts your approach as a parent. Maybe, if you really face it, you can best be described as a type A personality, someone with a need for order and control—sometimes at all costs (both of us are surely guilty of this).

Here is where you might want to bring in your partner (if you have one). Challenge one another to consider your competing or different parenting styles and to be honest in describing one another's defining characteristics. Ask yourself, are you a good cop or a bad cop? Maybe you're the patient parent—or maybe you've got the short fuse. Recently, my husband and I sat down to have an honest conversation about specific behaviors that we felt might negatively impact our kids, now or in the future. We each identified one behavior that we proactively wanted to work on. While it was slightly uncomfortable to admit our shortcomings as parents, it also gave each of us renewed motivation to be our best selves for our kids' well-being—and the opportunity to hold one another accountable. (Hint: one of us is currently working on not being so much of a neat freak.)

Maybe you are the one yelling at the opposing coach (or worse yet, your kid's own coach) from the sidelines at sports games, or maybe you are the one who can't stand the thought of someone disapproving of you. We challenge you to take a deep dive into who you are—the good, the bad, and the ugly.

If you're a single parent, most of the time the sole responsibility falls on you to address all child-rearing issues. If you can, find a trusted aunt, uncle, grandparent, teacher, or friend who may also assist you in the stickier, more gender-nuanced issues that arise in raising your child or in areas that are outside of your scope of talents or skills. Talk about behaviors to work on with them.

So why are we asking you to partake in this extensive self-reflection exercise at the very start of this book? After all, this is a book about parenting teenagers through a competitive and uncertain academic landscape. Why is deeply knowing yourself the first crucial step to practicing good parenting? We believe that the answer lies in the ancient proverb: "Physician heal thyself." Before you can effectively do any job that helps or influences others, you must first fix yourself. To throw in another idiom, don't be the pot calling the kettle black. In order to correct someone else, in this case your deeply beloved child, you had better be sure that you're also not exhibiting the same behaviors. You can parent with expertise and confidence if you and your partner (if applicable) are not only on the same page philosophically, but also if you both have participated in some deep, serious self-examination. In frank terms, you cannot heal a sickness or take good care of others without first being healed, in a healthy and clear headspace. Psychologist Madeline Levine cautions, "There is no parent more vulnerable to the excesses of over-parenting than an unhappy parent. One of the most important things we do for our children is to present them with a version of adult life that is appealing and worth striving for."[1] Parents, fix yourselves first.

At the end of this chapter you will find a helpful questionnaire for you to complete, preferably at the start of your teen's freshman year of high school (or, of course, whenever you get your hands on this book.) If you have a partner, we encourage you to separately answer the questions and discuss your results.

Then Know Your Child

Once you've considered who you are as a parent, it's time to examine each of your tween or teen children: temperament, gender, birth order, personality, gifts, skills that don't come naturally, and formative experiences. From the moment he or she was born, your son or daughter was a unique individual, bearing his or her own identity and genetic makeup. Some babies are quiet and wide eyed, eagerly taking in their surroundings as observers. Others are loud and verbal, making themselves known quite fiercely. And every combination of personality type exists in between. What's more, how a child begins behaving isn't always how he ends up, but sometimes we see some clues as to who he will become. As we all know, children are constantly changing, evolving, growing, challenging, and learning.

While most parents are not trained child psychologists, all parents can agree that each child comes out differently and with some qualities from her father and some from her mother. This, we know, is "nature." And "nurture" accounts for everything else we put into our children. How much attention we give them from a young age and how as parents we mellow or modify our styles based on our own life experiences and personal stages, all affect how they turn out. With the influences of nature and nurture, alongside birth order or gender of child and parent, no wonder each individual is just that: a distinct individual. And no wonder parenting is a hard, exhausting, evolving, ever-changing, and growing job. *But we believe that like most things in life, the more that you put in, the more you get out of it.*

Here's an author confession. I (Cynthia) have four children. The way my spouse and I parented our two younger children is different—not just based on birth order, but also based on parenting wisdom that we gained through experience, our changing energy levels, and our shifting values. My parent compass for my two younger teens is much less intense, less rigid, and frankly without sounding jaded, I care less about how things evolve because I know that at the back end of this journey everything—albeit hitting some walls of this parenting maze and redirecting along the way—*will* all work out. I am taking the long view. And also, I (like most of us I assume!) don't want my kids to be overly stressed out, or worse, suicidal, since I am now more keenly aware that they enjoy the journey more, live in the moment, and just do life as it unfolds. I think parents of multiple children can universally agree that over time our standards and priorities shift, and we place less emphasis on certain things that may have seemed really important with our first children and become much less so as we move through our parenting journey. I know that I am not alone in feeling more relaxed in my parenting as time marches on and that experience and wisdom gained replaces fear.

Make no mistake: encouraging you to embrace your parent compass must not be confused with adopting a laissez-faire attitude. Rather, we are advocating that you challenge your teen to be the very best he can be—but that you do it the right way, embracing fully who he uniquely is.

Appreciating Your Child Academically

Being realistic about where your teen fits academically within his school context is central to following a parent compass. Yes, we generally describe most of our kids as kind, bright, and hard working. But the reality is that some kids are naturally more academically inclined, push themselves (note that we said themselves, not you) to be the more accelerated honors and AP students, and rise to the top of their classes. While this race to the top has been coined a "Race to Nowhere"—an unhealthy ideal that's caused a mental health and suicide crisis—by the eponymous documentary, the reality remains that some students are just wired to enjoy school. But not all of them. In fact, most teens are just trying to stay afloat in a variety of high school-level courses, paired with all of the other academic and time pressures kids have lopped onto their over-scheduled afternoons and weekends. *Following your parent compass asks you to recognize, appreciate, and mentally and verbally support your children—no matter where they most naturally fall in the academic hierarchy of their schools.* Meet them at *their* place.

Do you feel your child could do better than where she naturally falls or has landed in her academic journey? Possibly. Maybe likely. We all want our kids to be the best version of themselves and the most academically "successful" that they are capable of being in order to meet their personal maximum potential. But we'd first implore you to examine what's at the root of pushing them, perhaps past what they can realistically handle. Do you fear judgment and rejection in your own journey? Could you be, perhaps, more concerned with how you appear to others as a parent than genuinely concerned about your teen's level of achievement? One head of school at a competitive college-prep high school (who wishes to remain anonymous) put it well when she reflected on her observations of today's parents: "The college process has become a competitive sport for parents and in their minds, is reflective of *their* own success as parents. If your child gets into a very competitive college or university, somehow you've raised [him or her] better than the other parents in your community."[2]

Somewhere in this complicated and competitive academic land-scape, *we as parents need to have the resolve to break the cycle of pushing our teens past their limit.* This pushing comes at a very high cost, and no family wants their teen to be the next statistic. So, parents, check yourselves. Restrain yourselves. You had your chance to be a student; now it is theirs, for better or for worse. Rather than nagging your teen, instead spend time with him on other activities such as reading together for pleasure in the same room, going on a walk, playing a game, or having a conversation about a topic that interests him. One of my student's intrigue of the stock market was an interest that his mother also shared.

Every morning over breakfast, they watched on television as the market opened and took in the news together. They didn't have to talk much; the shared experience was enough. Another student shared a deep enthusiasm for the same local professional sports team as his parent, making for a constant conversation topic whenever the team was in (or even off) season. Alongside eggs and toast, morning breakfasts consisted of reviewing scores and injured players and making predictions for the next games. Much more important for teens' mental health than pushing them is "[t]he quality of [the] relationship with their parents, [which] plays a critical role in the development of internalizing (stress, depression, etc.) and externalizing (alcohol, drug use, etc.) symptoms."[3] In addition, according to a recent study by the National Scientific Council on the Developing Child, you as a parent can directly impact your teen's academic experience by enriching her resilience. "Resilience results from a dynamic interaction between . . . an intrinsic resistance to adversity *and* strong relationships with important adults in [a teen's] family and community. Indeed, it is the *interaction* between biology and environment that builds the capacities to cope with adversity."[4] (We have more to say on resilience in Chapter 3.) Now isn't that the type of positive influence you'd rather practice, elevating your teen instead of adding to his already stressed-out existence?

Now Reconcile the Differences

It's once again time to reflect back on that composite of what your life was like when you were younger. Take some time now to thoughtfully and honestly compare that to what it would be like today. What is different about your teen's experience? Compare and contrast your experience with your impression of your teen's.

Here's the part where we're going to ask you to be brave. Have your child fill out the teen questionnaire that appears at the end of this chapter. Encourage him or her to be honest. And if she says, "I don't have time," or, "This is weird, Mom"? Tell her you want her to do this as a favor to you so that the two of you can get along better—that it is really important to you since you are trying to be a better parent. (Who can deny you that?) When she is done, share your questionnaires with one another, discussing the differences between your upbringing and hers. Talk about your strengths and your weaknesses, and allow yourself to be vulnerable enough to share some personal anecdotes so that you appear human and fallible, rather than the all-knowing, rule-enforcing parent. Then discuss your teen's strengths and weaknesses, your views on academics, and hers. Assure her that you will listen—just listen— while she reads her answers (and follow through with your promise, please). Parents, be courageous. Do not get defensive. (It will be a natural inclination, trust us.)

Our hope is that this exercise will not only open up lines of communication between you and your child, but also that it will give you some compassion for your teen's experience within the current competitive and uncertain academic landscape—one that might be very different from your own experience. As you work through the rest of the book, we encourage you to recall frequently the "physician heal thyself" concept. As you work toward reconciling the way you parent with the healthy habits of the parent compass, as you continue to refine your approach and understanding of your child's well-being, remember who you are and what got you here and contemplate how you are going to let that impact your future parenting.

During the course of the ensuing journey, you will likely have to sacrifice or put aside parental dreams in place of understanding your child as an individual in his or her journey. It's going to be hard. In today's future-thinking landscape, with many parents exhibiting early anxiety and forcibly paving the way for their kids' college careers, we have lost sight of the journey and instead focused too much on the destination. We implore you, fellow parents, to tweak your thinking in this way: rather than worrying about what your teen is not, instead celebrate the student that he is and accept that he will end up on a path that suits who he uniquely is.

Knowing Yourself Parent Questionnaire

Answer each question on your own, and ask your spouse or partner or other adult influencer in your child's life to reply to these, too. Share your replies and use them as discussion points *before* parenting your teen in high school academic and socioemotional-related issues. Your replies will serve as great conversation starters and will help you formulate a plan to practice better parenting behaviors.

1. What is your personal birth order? First, middle, last, or only child?

2. How were academics treated in your home when you were growing up? How is that different or similar to the way that academics are treated in your home now?

3. Reflect on your own relationship with your parents. How would you characterize it, and what are you doing to imitate (or distance yourself from) that parenting style?

4. Did you feel stereotyped or labeled by your parents (and possibly in comparison to your siblings)? How did that affect you? Was it helpful? Harmful? Something you were proud of or tried to conceal?

5. What is your personal high school and college educational background? Private versus public high school? If you went to college, what kind of college? Private? Public? Community? Close to home? Far away? Transferred schools? Trade school? Did you join the military?

6. In a few sentences or words, describe your personality in high school (i.e., socially connected or anti-social, nerdy or cool/popular, leader or follower) and your personality now.

7. In a sentence or two, describe the kind of academic student you were in high school (i.e., independent learner; highly self-motivated; on the lazier side; confident in some but not all classes; honors/AP student or regular-track student; great,

average, or poor test taker; shy or a self-advocate with teachers; didn't like, liked, or loved school; math/science or humanities/language arts preference; well-rounded or pointy).

8. What did you think you wanted to study when you started college versus what your final major(s) was/were?

9. Was your college experience what you expected (e.g., socially, academically)? Were you satisfied with it? Were you well prepared socially and academically? Did you have any regrets?

10. Did your parents pay for college? Did you take out loans or participate in work study? Did you have financial aid? How and when were you or your family able to pay off college, if necessary?

11. What is one thing you can do better or change in order to best support your child?

12. What is one thing your spouse (if applicable) can do better or change in order to best support your child?

Knowing Yourself Teen Questionnaire

1. What are generally your favorite subjects and who are your favorite teachers? (This may change from year to year, so record your current favorites.) Have any subjects that you used to like become "ruined" by teachers you don't connect with? Or do you have new subjects that you like due to an amazing and inspiring teacher?

2. What activities do you enjoy doing after school and on weekends? (These can be anything from academic to purely recreational.) Do you do any of these to please your parent(s), or are they self-selected?

3. What do you wish your parents knew about you and school?

4. What do you wish your parents would stop doing in relation to you or your school and/or activities?

5. Do you have any tutors? Does it feel like too much? Too little? Necessary? A waste of time? Can you wean off of tutors in any classes?

6. What is one thing your parent(s) can do to help make your homework or school experience more productive?

7. When do you have time to have chats or weekly calendar/life/ update conversations with your parents (e.g., during snack/ meals or before bed)?

8. Do you feel stressed or anxious? If so, please describe your feelings and how you have dealt with them to your parents.

9. What have you found is effective in helping to cope with or relieve your stress? Is there anything you want your parents to understand about how you cope with stress?

10. What do you like to do to decompress and relax?

11. Would you describe yourself as a generally happy person? Stressed? Outgoing? A leader, follower, or joiner? Other adjectives?

Following your parent compass is a practice and discipline that requires checking yourself often, pivoting when necessary, and improvising along the way, all backed by tools and strategies that will help your teen stay happy and healthy while you consult and cheerlead on the sidelines. The grueling work of self-examination coupled with applying and personalizing your parenting style with each of your individual children will contribute to your children feeling understood. When you are able to model to your kids humility and honesty about who you are and what makes you parent the way that you do, chances are they will start to open up to you, too—and therein lies the first step toward a more harmonious and happier relationship.

CHAPTER 3:

PRAISE THE JOURNEY, NOT THE DESTINATION

Marco skipped kindergarten. I knew this fact because his mother made sure to tell me at our first meeting as soon as she settled into the tan leather couch directly opposite me. My knowledge was reinforced just minutes later when she proudly handed me his résumé; right there at the top, under "Education," it was hard to miss the special note indicating that Marco had indeed jumped from Pre-K straight into first grade. Marco's mother beamed with pride. I gulped.

Yet Marco and his mother sat in my office because Marco was, according to his mother, unmotivated. During our meeting, Marco's mother pointed out over and over again how smart her son was, but Marco was an average student and, per his mother's complaints, refused to explore his interests in a meaningful way outside of the classroom. Instead, much to his mother's dismay, he was exploring the world of video games far too often. During the course of our conversation, it became clear to me that Marco knew he was smart—his mother had been telling him so his whole life. But in doing so, Marco's mother was in fact influencing his motivation (or demotivation, as it were). You see, being smart had become Marco's identity. This young man avoided challenging himself inside and outside of class and never developed a zest for exploration (and instead adopted an arrogant attitude to boot), largely due to this "smart" label.

The Growth Mindset

I've seen this phenomenon time and time again—kids who have been told they're smart for as long as they can remember, and as a result, they don't exhibit grit or effort either because they don't want to ruin their "smart" reputation or because they figure they are already smart and therefore don't need to improve. This observation is backed up by research. In her work, researcher and psychologist Carol Dweck has spent decades examining the *growth mindset* versus the *fixed mindset* and how they impact student motivation. A *growth mindset* is one wherein a student believes that intelligence can be built upon—improved over time—and that hard work, coupled with taking away lessons for improvement and utilizing self-advocacy skills, can result in greater knowledge. A *fixed mindset*, on the other hand, is when a student approaches the world from the standpoint that his intelligence is a fixed concept—he is either smart or he is not; intelligence doesn't change and therefore extra effort cannot affect it. Dweck found that students who have adopted a growth mindset are better adjusted and more resilient and, in turn, accomplish more academically. Those who have a fixed mindset, afraid to undermine their label as "smart," tend to shy away from embracing challenge and taking risks that stretch themselves.[1]

The Making Caring Common Project, an initiative out of the Harvard Graduate School of Education, conducted a study looking at the messages that parents are sending to their children. The researchers surveyed more than 10,000 middle and high school students. They found that those students were, not surprisingly, three times more likely to agree than disagree with the following: "My parents are prouder if I get good grades in my classes than if I am a caring community member in class and school." (What was just as disheartening to learn was that 80 percent of respondents believed that their parents valued personal happiness and achievement over caring for others.)[2]

Indeed, many of the kids we've seen in our offices place a premium on maintaining a certain grade point average (GPA). Parents frantically call or email when they think their child's GPA might be ever-so-mildly affected by the smallest of infractions. As a result, we routinely see students who take less challenging classes than they are capable of taking because they wish to perpetuate an image of "the straight-A student." They mistakenly think that taking less challenging classes will result in a high GPA and that they will be at an advantage over their peers (even those who choose harder classes) with lower GPAs. Parents, let us assure you: admission officers look at the classes chosen within the context of each individual applicant's school and the trends and patterns in grades through the years—not a straight GPA in a vacuum. And if that means taking the more challenging class and earning less than an "A," so be it. In the process, your child will learn what it is to work hard, make mistakes and get off track, and fine-tune adjustments accordingly.

Carol Dweck epitomizes the point we are trying to make in the following observation: "If parents want to give their children a gift, the best they can do is to teach their children to love challenges, be intrigued by mistakes, enjoy effort, and keep on learning . . . We can ask them about their work in a way that appreciates and admires their effort and choices."[3]

An Instagram Post

A couple of months ago, I came across the casual Instagram post of an acquaintance. This mom proudly posted a photo of her beaming daughter, who was equally as proudly displaying her brand-new kitten. Sure, it was cute, but that's not what grabbed my attention. The unsuspecting daughter was still in her swimsuit, having finished a swim meet earlier in the day. In her caption, the mom offered a rundown of how the day had unfolded. She had bribed her daughter with this reward if the child (who was a mere eight years old!) won her heat at her swim meet. Well, guess what? The child won her race, so mom did what all noble parents do and kept her promise. I remember feeling a little queasy as I read through the post—like I wanted to shake the mom and divulge all things parenting compass. Parents, a reward for a job well done is fine and can most definitely be part of your parenting repertoire. But a bribe to produce a goal or a medal only perpetuates the "outcome over effort" mentality. Please, parents, we implore you— check yourselves.

Doing Hard Things

One of the best ways that we can help our kids learn resilience is to watch them do hard things, even if we know they are going to fail or falter, and then support them if they don't succeed. I don't know about you, but even from the time my kids were little, it was excruciating to watch them struggle as they learned a new task or concept: tying their shoes, making their bed. Sometimes, it felt easier (and quicker!) to simply do it for them. Of course, the types of tasks become more complicated and have more consequences over time. But the bottom line remains the same: the trouble inherent in the message that we send to our children by swooping in to save the day, no matter the task, is that they can't do it themselves. We set the bar too low. So, guess what our rescuing behavior is inadvertently telling them to do? (Answer: likewise to set the bar too low.)

The reality is that encouraging and watching our kids do hard things (our own fingernail biting and wincing aside) is exactly what propels them forward, teaches them grit and discipline, and—in the future—will help them to see the positive side of a setback. I remember once, years ago, asking one of my especially high-achieving and well-adjusted students what she felt her parents did that supported her in getting to where she was. Without hesitation, she remarked (verbatim), "They made me do hard things." That exchange has always stuck with me. Indeed, during our interview with Dr. Michael Dennin, Vice Provost for Teaching and Learning at the University of California–Irvine, we asked him about the single most important thing that parents of high schoolers should know. Resolutely, he advised: "It is important to understand how to develop a true growth mindset in students. They need to see problems as opportunities for growth and creative solutions. They need to understand that some things are worth the hard work to get better at it and that even doing poorly on assignments and school work at times is a necessary step to learning and getting better."[4]

What does doing hard things look like? It looks different for every kid, but universally it involves the tasks that don't come easily to them.

It looks like struggle, frustration, and often an urge to give up. And fundamentally, your role as a parent in facilitating your child's ability to "do hard things" is to encourage her to push through despite the pain and tediousness of mastery, signaling that you support her but are not going to do it for her.

Making Mistakes and Embracing Growth Potential

About Sam

Let's examine a student who has been honing his ability to make mistakes—and to learn from them—for nearly his whole life. Sam's drive was notably exceptional. Sam's parents understood that the best way to parent him was to recognize his effort, discuss improvement strategy when a mistake was made, and allow him to explore his curiosities. Sam and I were chatting one day about his academic journey, and I noticed that many of his stories were in fact failures or mistakes that he had made. But what was the most intriguing thing to me was that Sam described those mistakes with appreciation for where they led him. First there was the time when his self-built remote-controlled airplane crashed when he was a young kid. Disappointed initially that its inaugural flight was unsuccessful (and seeing his hard-earned chore money literally come crashing down), he quickly found instead that he relished in rebuilding it, focusing in particular on identifying and then rectifying the deficiencies of the previous model. (I should say models, because he did it again and again until he got it right.) Then there was the time that he was not satisfied with his progress in his English class, having earned a couple of poor grades on his papers. He committed to visiting his teacher's tutorial after every exam or paper, focusing on what he did not do correctly. He worked out a deal with her to write extra essays in addition to those assigned to the class to practice his skills and to get her feedback on his style. Low and behold, the effort paid off; his writing vastly improved, and he earned an A in the class. Next there was the time in violin that he simply could not master the level of improvisation expected of him, try as he might. His frustration was significant. But instead of throwing in the towel (which he did consider), he chose to devise a step-by-step plan that, over time, would allow him to perfect the complicated note sequences he sought to master.

And then he recalled his journey with computer science. Thrilled by the power of coding but nervous to undertake the challenge and tedium, Sam dipped his toes into it, but beyond "hello world," when his computer screen was rife with error messages, he became discouraged. He recruited a close friend to help him over the hurdle, and together, with tunnel vision, they created. Before the end of his senior year, he had gained two internships at tech startups, had created not one but two of his own startups, and in college is diligently working toward his goal to create a large-scale startup utilizing artificial intelligence. Sam had not taken a direct road to get where he was. Instead, he had experienced some setbacks and made some mistakes, which refined his path and enabled him to explore, then used the knowledge to propel his next steps. But ultimately, the journey led him to some incredible places.

About Aryan

The most striking thing about Aryan was where he resolutely chose to place his daily focus. Aryan was a student who, I couldn't help but notice, had mastered the art of fixating not on his areas of strength, but on his areas of growth—and with an uncanny, laser-sharp focus. Aryan naturally saw his intelligence as something that could grow with him. There were many things that Aryan could do quite well: painting, writing, music. But that's not where he spent most of his time. Aryan knew that in order to achieve the lofty goals he had set for himself, he needed to instead vastly improve upon what he called his "deficiencies." He did this as a practice. One of his "deficiencies" was computer science, which did not come naturally to him. But in order to get closer to his goal of developing and marketing unique, life-changing devices, he needed to master computer science—so that's what he did. Sometimes his grades in his computer science classes weren't what he wanted them to be, but those lower marks taught him valuable lessons. He spent countless, painstaking hours researching on his own time to learn how to code and to master more and more programming languages, and he even chose to major in computer science for the purpose of becoming better at something that did not come naturally to him. Aryan had cultivated a growth mindset; to him, his intelligence was not a fixed concept but rather grew as he fed it.

Both Sam and Aryan, with the help of supportive parents, worked toward their goals with grit and resilience in the face of challenge, because they saw their "smartness" as something that could improve: what they put in, they got out tenfold. Neither of these young men was overly concerned with how it looked to others if a remote-controlled plane crashed over and over again or if a difficult subject resulted in obvious struggle until he got it right; instead, they were more concerned with the process of learning and, in turn, were able to work diligently toward their goals. And perhaps most importantly, when they faltered, they analyzed their mistakes. They thought through what they saw as areas of growth and came up with ways to improve in those areas. They added the word "yet" to their acknowledgment of deficiencies rather than made excuses. That is, they said to themselves, "I'm not good at that . . . yet."[5]

Recovering from Failure

If you find yourself able to watch your kid do hard things, chances are, he is going to fail from time to time. So how do you support him when the inevitable happens?

- Analyze the mistake or failure and help your teen develop an action plan for moving forward. Simply praising the effort isn't enough. While it's a start, figuring out why it happened and how to move forward to *improve* is a critical, and often overlooked, next step.[6]

- Ask your child to identify two positive outcomes of the failure. If she has difficulty, offer a suggestion.

- Discuss the lesson to employ next time.

- Pull out an example of a massive failure of your own. Talk about what you learned and where it led you.

- Help him identify someone or something that can help him learn more about this task or subject.

- Remind your teen that how she recovers from the failure is even more important than the setback itself. What she chooses to do with the hard lesson learned (i.e., get up and dust herself off, win the ball the next time she is knocked down, or try again and again) is in and of itself evidence of growth and persistence in the journey.

- Realize that some teen stress and anxiety (in moderation) is not all bad. Experiencing some heightened feelings when preparing for or taking a test, or before giving a public presentation or performance, for example, actually helps students do better! Natural surges of adrenaline can make us perform at a higher level and even fuel us to conquer our own fears and anxiety, too, often resulting in increased resilience. So parents, don't try to minimize or, worse, eliminate stress for your teen altogether. Allow them to sit in it, knowing that moderate stress and anxiety is not always a bad thing.[7]

- Find some humor (if it is not too painful). Failure can sometimes (but not always) be something you can laugh about later.

- Reiterate these adages, "When one door closes a window opens," "view the cup half full instead of empty," and "make lemons out of lemonade." The more you model positivity, the more likely your teen will be to embrace a similar mindset. (As an added bonus, when your teen starts to practice this type of positivity on his own, his attitude could very well impact those around him, inspiring friends and peers to approach challenges in a similar fashion.)

Remarks a headmaster addressing parents at his school:

We're often asked by parents, "What can I do? How can I be helpful and not a hindrance?" The best you can do for your children during the process is to normalize struggle and imperfection and to remind them, in various ways, you love them unconditionally. In the face of disappointing news, remember the wise words of Brené Brown: "Together we will cry and face fear and grief. I will want to take away your pain. But instead I will sit with you and teach you how to feel it." Remind your children they are not defined by outcomes, and that you will love them the exact same way no matter what. That's the best care they could receive.[8]

Becoming a Self-Advocate

Part of learning to make mistakes is developing the ability to learn from them. But what happens when we aren't sure how to proceed from the point of the mistake? This is where self-advocacy comes in. Part of your job should be to encourage your child to seek help and advice when she needs it. Bad grade on a test? Meet with the teacher to fully understand the mistakes made and to learn what could have been done better. Robot failed to complete a challenge in competition? Seek out a mentor or coach to help understand where the code failed. Want to see a change on campus? Ask for it or lead it. Self-advocacy is a critical piece to the growth mindset puzzle.

But the problem is that many young people have not had enough opportunities to practice self-advocacy. Snowplow parents have groomed the path straight down to the tundra, and the affected kids haven't been forced to identify a need or, much less, ask for it themselves. As a result of overbearing, non-compass following parents, for many teens, approaching others for help is too intimidating, and constructive feedback is too scary. But the reality is that this type of feedback is both common and indeed necessary to our growth as human beings; allow your child to sit in the discomfort and disappointment of hard-to-hear constructive criticism before you dive in to eliminate his pain for him. Fellow parents, you can encourage your teen over time to discuss his mistakes and to learn from them. You can walk alongside him as he identifies his problems and develops appropriate action plans. You can help him, even from a very early age, learn that he has a voice and that it is valued.

From the time my kids could talk, I encouraged them to speak up for themselves. If we were out at a restaurant and they wanted a coloring sheet and crayons to pass the time, they knew that they needed to ask the host for them. (I sure didn't want to color a picture of a giraffe, so I wasn't going to ask for it.) When it came time to order food, they practiced using their voice, telling the server what they wanted to eat. When they were thirsty, they had to ask the server for a refill of water. As time went on, they learned to tell the doctor what hurt. Eventually, each time they "tried on" self-advocacy skills, the fact that they had a voice was reinforced—they had practiced it day in and day out. Even teens sometimes don't place their own orders at a restaurant or ask for a drink refill because their hovering, enabling parents jump in to do it for them. Please don't. No matter how old your kids are, you can instill in them self-advocacy skills. Here are a few ideas to get you started:

- Show personal restraint and keep your mouth shut in settings where you and your teen are with another adult or expert (e.g., teacher, doctor, manager, meal server), and gesture to your teen to do the talking.

- Practice role-playing at home with your teen if he has to go in to speak to a teacher or administrator about a concern or issue. Then circle back when he is home from school by asking how it went.

- Praise your teen's self-advocacy efforts. When you witness her speaking up on behalf of herself, a sibling, a friend, or even you, thank her and acknowledge her assertiveness.

In a recent *Grown and Flown* article, a mother reflects on her experience allowing her son to self-advocate. She was used to jumping in to "fix things," and when her son had an issue with a bully, she immediately went into "mother hen mode," frantically brainstorming all of the ways that she could help him by intervening: email the teacher for him, set up a meeting, then move to Plan B. The son stopped her mid-brainstorm and softly said, "Mom, I'm not asking you to fix it. I just want to talk with you about it." She stumbled for a moment as she realized that he was right—her job was to listen, not to fix. His job was to self-advocate. The next day when her son came home from school, she recalls, "He was so proud of himself . . . when he told me how he handled it. *He fixed it—he did it, not me.* The way it should be. What if he hadn't spoken up? In my effort to help, I would have ruined any chance for him to take care of himself. How many times had he subtly tried to tell me this before? How many times have our children sat there while we rambled on with solutions when all they really wanted was for someone to listen? He taught me such a valuable lesson—he taught me to stop and listen. Instead of 'I've got this,' I had to learn 'You've got this.'" She went on to reflect upon their ensuing journey together and ultimately the close, trusting relationship that they forged—one in which he articulated that he truly felt his opinion mattered, as a result of her practiced ability to sit back and let him solve his own problems. Fellow parents, follow a parent compass lesson from this mother-son duo.[9]

One Final Observation

As I was writing this chapter and rereading it (and rereading it, and rereading it), I was struck with the number of times the words "pride" and "proud" appeared in the text. I later replaced some mentions of these words with synonyms, but even so, five appearances of some form of the word "proud" still made the cut. It got me thinking about what's at the core of praising outcome over effort: trophies, public recognition, spotlights, certificates, gold stars—even kittens. Have we gotten so off track that we truly do value achievement over kindness, generosity, effort, and citizenship? If not, parents, then please check your pride and make more intentional parenting choices. Ask yourself about the message you are sending to your kids when you laud what they achieve over what it takes for them to get there.

CHAPTER 4:

HELP YOUR TEEN PURSUE INTERESTS AND PURPOSE

When Grace was nine years old, her parents took her to the circus for her birthday. That was the day that she fell in love with the flying trapeze. Every day that followed, Grace begged and pleaded for lessons so that she could learn to fly. Her parents had absolutely no idea how to expose their daughter to this foreign hobby. But Grace couldn't stop dreaming about flying just like the performers; she pored over every trapeze YouTube video she could find and even enlisted her brother to help her construct a makeshift swing in the backyard. Grace's parents considered it their duty to try to provide an experience for Grace's obsession, despite their fear that she wouldn't like it once she tried it. To their surprise, after hours of research, they found some summer camps that offered circus components; the day Grace hooked up to her harness was the beginning of her long trapeze career. She attended circus camp every summer, watched Cirque du Soleil shows live and on YouTube, and even located a vacation destination for her family that offered trapeze lessons. She applied to colleges with her "pointy" interest, making sure that her college choices were located near to a gym where she could continue to hone her craft.

See Your Child

Parents, one of your primary goals in following your parent compass should be to truly see your child—*the child you have, not the child you want to inauthentically create.* We concede that it sure sounds simple, but in reality takes a great deal of time, patience, observation, tinkering, and humility alongside good partnering with your spouse (or other single parents and extended family) along the way. It involves listening and genuinely hearing what your child is telling you, whether explicit or not. Professor of Psychiatry Daniel J. Siegel and psychotherapist Tina Payne Bryson, authors of *The Power of Showing Up* and *The Whole-Brain Child*, write:

> You know the clichés of the dad who pushes his disinterested son to be an athlete, or the mom who rides her child to make straight A's, regardless of the child's inclinations. These are parents failing to see who their kids really are. If they happen occasionally over the course of a childhood, they won't make a huge difference—no one can truly see a child 100 percent of the time. But over time the child's sense of not being seen can not only harm the child, but the parent and the relationship.
>
> That sets up a heartbreaking reality: there are kids who live a majority of their childhoods not being seen. Never feeling understood. Rarely having the experience that someone feels their feelings, takes on their perspective, knows their likes and dislikes. Imagine how these children feel—invisible and alone. When they think about their teachers, their peers, even their parents, one thought can run through their minds: "They don't get me at all."[1]

Recently, I met with a young student whose mother confided in me on the phone before the meeting. She had been expressly concerned that her son, Matthew, was "lazy" (her words, not mine). Trish complained to me that her sophomore wasn't interested in *any* activities outside of the classroom, and she was deeply frustrated when it came to helping him identify ways to "appropriately" spend his free time. Armed with this background information, I was really interested in getting to know Matthew and trying to identify what truly made him "tick"—it's my experience that typically something is there. During our session, admittedly Matthew did have some difficulty identifying what got him excited about his classes at school. But that's when we moved on to goal setting (see Chapter 7 for our unabashed support for goal setting). While goals one and two came a bit slowly, when it came time to set goal number three, Matthew knew immediately that goal three should be dedicated to the improvement of his cooking skills. While he had been somewhat reserved during our session up until that point, all of a sudden Matthew came alive, gushing about the recipes he had tried (and failed), those he had nailed, and those he planned to test out before the approaching Thanksgiving holiday. He told me about the cooking class he had researched online that he planned to take with his mom (which she obviously conveniently forgot about when she told me he was lazy). I realized that all Matthew needed was the freedom to talk about what really got *him* excited. Parents, here is a tip: if your child's interest isn't strictly "academic," indulge him anyway. The benefits could be immense—and even unexpected. He will learn not only to listen to his gut, but also that you *hear* him—that you *trust* his instinct. What's more, you never know where his interest will lead. Maybe a cursory interest in cooking will lead him to explore the delectable and scientific world of molecular gastronomy (true story—I've seen it happen). Or maybe it will lead to an audition on a junior chef reality television show (true story, too). And won't you want to be sitting—and tasting—in that delicious test kitchen?

The first step to facilitating your child's interests is to expose her to as much as you can, whether thoughtful ideas, academic pursuits, or extracurricular activities such as sports, art, community service, or religion. If we really challenge ourselves to listen, our kids start to indicate the things they most enjoy and generally show some enthusiasm and passion for certain areas. Once you see these interests emerge—even if their natural skills don't seem to be too strong in these areas—fuel and facilitate more of them. If the activities seem to genuinely excite them, run with it.

Be careful here: it is easy to let our own biases and wishes *for them* creep in. I am certainly not immune to this misstep. One of my daughters begged for ballet lessons seemingly from the moment she could speak. When she encountered music that ever-so-remotely resembled "ballet music," the urge to dance overtook her little body, and she'd sashay around the room. A swimmer and volleyball player myself, I stubbornly wanted her to turn toward similar sports—but you know what? That wasn't her thing. Only after she implored my husband to build her a life-size ballet barre that she could keep in her room for daily practice did it dawn on me that I needed to practice what I preached, and we started to explore the unfamiliar (to me) world of dance. Parents, do you see yourself in this experience?

There is no right or wrong, no preconceived, rote profile in the eyes of colleges. Whatever makes a student tick is what schools want to know about. An entire class full of computer scientists wouldn't make any sense. But a class comprised of computer scientists, trapeze artists, molecular gastronomists, tuba players, entrepreneurs, bioengineers, event planners, World War II aficionados, ballerinas, and gerontologists? Now that's interesting. And that builds a diverse and intentional community—diverse in interests, ethnicities, socio-economic backgrounds and more—something that college admission officers try to achieve when building a class. *Don't get suckered into thinking that one way is the right way or the only way or what colleges are "looking for." Pushing your kids into an interest or activity because you believe—or someone told you—it will "look good" for college is never a reason to force your teen into doing something.* And frankly, that approach goes against everything that we are trying to teach in *The Parent Compass*. Honestly, how would you like to show up every day to a job at which you didn't have the freedom to exercise your strengths or to have a career that your parents dreamed you would have (rather than the one you dreamed about)? Parents, take the time to expose your kids to different recreational and extracurricular or academic activities, and see what sticks. And remember: life's goal does not need to be the Olympics, a college athletic scholarship, or a future professional sports endeavor. Help your teen pursue what she enjoys and you will by default be following your parent compass.

Activities Are for Growth and Enjoyment

When supporting your teen's extracurricular interests—which by now you should know may very well not line up with your own—realize that his interests may be just about anything: school sports teams or clubs, volunteer organizations, religious activities, performing or fine arts, or academic activities such as robotics, research, speech and debate, Model United Nations, mock trial, other academic endeavors, and even an off-the-beaten-path hobby (remember trapeze-loving Grace?). Tutoring, by the way, is *not* an extracurricular activity! When consulting with your teen as he participates in the activities that bring him pleasure, *understand that they are done for your teen's growth and enjoyment.* This doesn't mean that the activities have to be fun and engaging every step of the way (and we support teens doing hard or boring tasks because, hey, life is sometimes that way), and they may be rigorous and taxing at times, but overall these activities should be enjoyable.

About Jack

I remember a session with parents who told me about their older son, Jack. Jack had pointed enthusiastically at airplanes before he could speak. His eyes would light up as he gestured toward the sky, squealing with delight, practically jumping from his mother's arms upward every time he saw a plane. As the years progressed, Jack's father took his son to watch airplanes take off from the airport; his mother toured airplane museums with him. They subscribed to aviation magazines, checked out library books about planes, and went to movies and watched TV shows with airplanes in them, and when he was old enough, his parents allowed him to get flying lessons. In college, Jack studied physics, and now, he—not surprisingly—has become a pilot.

About Nate

Jack's younger brother, Nate, was quite the opposite. He liked to try many things whether academic clubs, athletics, community service, or summer employment. He was more like a "Jack-of-all-trades" than a Nate. His parents were concerned that his interests were too varied and all over the place. But when I asked Nate about his full calendar of extracurricular activities, he told me that he couldn't and wouldn't give up any of them. "They each excite me. And they bring out different parts of me." Unless these activities were somehow harming his classroom focus or putting a strain on his sleep or grades, I didn't see any reason that he had to give any of them up. What did Nate go on to do in college? Two majors and a minor—and more activities, too! Nate was a kid who liked to juggle a lot. Two brothers. Same parents. Totally different sons with very different styles and interests. Jack and Nate's parents allowed them both to pursue their independent interests.

Jack's trajectory is what we call "pointy," certain of a passion and almost monomaniacal in pursuing it. But it isn't always that clear and often takes time to see how interests evolve. Nate, on the other hand, is more well-rounded. Some kids like to try on a lot of activities and never decide upon just one. But as parents following a compass, we need to be in tune with what does excite and enthuse our kids, even if it is a very different interest from our own. Pushing kids to do what we want them to do doesn't always work out, as we have seen over and over again in our years working with teens and families; in fact, doing so almost inevitably leads to burnout and, worse, resentment and discord in your relationship with your teen.

Values

When your teen starts to explore her interests, you may want to start having conversations about values. Ask her what she values and, more importantly, help her put names to those values. Indeed, we've found that most junior high and high school students haven't had the opportunity to explicitly identify their own personal values (and they are different for every one of us!), yet values should be the driving force behind everything from time management and prioritization to activities selection and even classroom learning. Does she value integrity? Achievement? Loyalty? Commitment? Perhaps she values adventure or family. Talk to her often about purpose. *Our core values should drive the choices that we make, and when they don't, we feel unfulfilled.* So parents: show restraint. Remember, you had your turn to pursue your middle and high school purpose. Now, you are just along for the ride, facilitating when appropriate and helping to navigate the ups and downs along the way.

Choosing Activities

Fellow parents, you should be seated in the back seat as opposed to maneuvering the steering wheel when it comes to how your teen spends time outside of school. Ask yourself how many of your child's activities you have selected or pushed versus the number that he wanted to explore. If your answer is that you have orchestrated your teen's extracurricular activities, then please get back on track in understanding your role.

Navigating Sports with a Compass

Do you remember your teen son wearing his tiny soccer jersey that hung below his thighs playing three-on-three soccer—and all six little players swarming around the ball like bumble bees? Or your daughter in her much-too-big tae kwon do outfit collecting taped stripes or a stamp on her belt for each class she attended? How about the first time he wore a much-too-big and wobbly football helmet or she swung a tee-ball bat and hit the rubber neck of the tee? Whether you exposed your teen to many or just a few sports in his or her childhood, chances are that eventually societal pressures and a packed schedule dictated the necessity to specialize in just one or two sports for what seems to be an exorbitant amount of time. A generation ago we played multiple sports for our local communities and schools. And sports were not year-round and did not limit kids from participating in multiple sports, even when they overlapped seasons. Now, as we know, youth sports are much different.

Don't get us wrong. We believe that athletics teach invaluable life lessons and that physical fitness, in some form, should indeed be a part of every teen's routine. No one can deny that sports engender hustle and leadership, sportsmanship and respect—all things that translate to experiences beyond the field and, indeed, beyond the teenage years. But we have also witnessed how out of hand teen sports can become. We are not advocating that your teen quit sports or, worse, not try them at all. Instead, in this section, our intention is to challenge you to think realistically about the role competitive athletics have in your teen's life, and we are asking you to reflect on the impact that you have on your teen's experience.

Have you heard about author Malcolm Gladwell's pronouncement of the magic 10,000 hours required to excel in a sport? Perhaps a better question is, have you pushed your child into racking up those 10,000 hours—even when it isn't his dream, but yours? How many of you have gently (or not so gently) pushed your child into a sport that is a college admission strategic sport (whether the more obscure fencing or discus throwing, the popular and rather elite crew or sailing, or a soccer club as opposed to a recreational team)? And at what cost has this come, both literally in terms of dollars and in terms of time committed and injuries sustained?

We feel compelled to address the fine line here. We believe that parents must support their kids in the endeavors that *the kids* have selected and enjoy. Additionally, parenting with a compass does not support pushing children to the point of emotional or physical exhaustion. Yes, there will be pressure-filled days, and yes, there will be weeks of exhausting practices—and we are firm believers in urging kids to stick firmly to their commitments and to push through challenging situations. It is in those very low times that parents have to read between the lines to ensure that their teen's mental health is intact and that their teen is still glad she is doing the activity—despite these hard days and weeks. During those trying times, practice parent etiquette; offer a shoulder to cry on, be a sounding board, cheerlead, and listen. *Restrain yourself from being a "fixer"; instead listen to your teen as she navigates how to fix her own problems.*

Statistics prove that "overall a little over 7 percent of high school athletes (about 1 in 14) [go] on to play a varsity sport in college and less than 2 percent of high school athletes (1 in 54) [go] on to play at NCAA Division I schools."[2] (And for those very curious parents who simply need a good dose of reality, this note will lead you to a chart that divides up these odds by sport.)[3] Overall, for the time (and financial resources) put into sports teams, coaches, and games, and the weekends, vacations, and celebrations sacrificed due to sports conflicts, the numbers are pretty low to become college capable or viable athletes. And what's more, what happens when your teen has early burn-out, no longer likes the sport even though he shows a talent or skill, or experiences an injury such as a concussion or surgery that prevents him from continuing? *Turn off the outside noise, put in your literal or proverbial earplugs* (more on those in Chapter 9), *and get in touch with your teen about whether his sport is really worth all of the physical, emotional, and financial sacrifice.*

In the HBO *Real Sports* segments hosted by Bryant Gumbel, one particular episode looks at the huge increase in youth sports injuries that have escalated over the last ten years as a result of the current generation of kids specializing in one sport, year round, for too many hours per week. Orthopedic surgeons communicate concerns about a trend in the "professionalization in youth sports that is now upwards of a 19 billion dollar a year industry in the United States." Orthopedic "research has shown that the number of ACL [knee ligament] reconstructions on children and adolescents had spiked nearly five times in just a decade."[4] The overuse of growing bones and muscles from required year-round sports participation has turned the mostly adult patient base of many orthopedic doctors into a client stream of tween and teen patients. This series interviews teens and their parents in a poignant segment that we believe every parent of an adolescent competitive athlete should be required to watch. What has happened to the youth recreational sports teams in our country, or even many school sports teams? They have lost so many of their athletes to pay-to-play clubs; private coaches; and elite, specialized athletic training centers. And it has come at a cost—physically, mentally, and financially.

It's a fact that athletics consume a lot of time. Most in-school and outside-of-school coaches demand students to show up to all practices and often take away playing time for those who don't. This puts teens in a tough position if they have a doctor's appointment after school, a huge test the day after a practice, or a mild injury that they try to play through so that they don't lose their coveted team spot or playing time. This is where parents following their compasses can greatly help their teens, but not in the way that you might expect. *Do not pick up the phone to call, email, or speak face-to-face with a coach before or after practice.* That is not your job. Instead, *help equip your teen to self-advocate.* If there is an issue of concern about time, mental or physical health, or grades slipping due to participation on a sports team, have your teen speak with the coach directly and sincerely. There really should not be a reason beyond middle school that a parent speaks to a coach. High school students must learn to self-advocate.

And parents, please be realistic. If your child is not being recruited to play in college or doesn't show Olympic-level promise (which is the case for the majority of kids), don't expect that with hundreds of hours of extra coaching your teen will "break through." Allow her to enjoy the fun and learn the life lessons that come with those athletic experiences: teamwork, resilience, showing respect (to teammates, coaches, the other team, and referees), and hustle. Youth sports are meant to be fun and recreational and are not meant to fuel (mostly) false hopes of becoming a college athlete.

So, parents, follow these dos and don'ts regarding your teen in athletics:

- Do have fun enjoying the privilege of watching your kid play and learn great life lessons on the field.

- Do cheer positively when good things happen or encourage when your teen needs a lift.

- Do volunteer to bring snacks, oranges, drinks, or a team treat.

- Do pitch in on a coach gift at the end of each season for every sport your kid plays.

- Do allow the coaches to do their job and coach. Remember that you are not the coach (unless you want to become one!).

- Do thank the coach and the referees and encourage your child to do the same after every game.

- Do clap for both teams at the end of the game, the team that wins and the team that loses, no matter which team your teen is on.

- Don't yell at the referee, coach, or other players or attempt to coach from the sidelines. If you know you have a problem with this directive, ask a trusted other to keep you in check.

- Don't shout out comments other than positive ones to either team.

- Don't get kicked out of a game for having bad sideline behavior (we have seen it happen and have heard about it more times than you might realize).

- Don't be the parent who embarrasses your kid, team, or community by acting with improper etiquette.

- Don't offer criticism of any player on your teen's team or the other team, including your own teen.

We love the reminder signs posted on the sidelines of sports fields that read, "Before you complain, have you volunteered yet?" or, "Please remember: these are kids. This is a game. The coaches are volunteers. The umpires are human. This is not professional baseball."[5] Many sports teams now have parent conduct codes that parents must sign before a child can participate, and we support these valuable pledges. Some middle and high schools even have a twenty-four-hour rule whereby parents cannot contact a coach within twenty-four hours before or after any game. It offers a buffer before games to dissuade attempts to influence (or threaten) a coach and also allows a cool-off period after what may or may not have happened during a game. There is a progressing general awareness to practice good behavior before, during, and after sporting events, so please, contribute to helping this movement grow in the right direction.

About Chris

Our family met Chris while on vacation. He was an only child and a high school junior, traveling with his parents. We happened to be on the same small tour, and over lunch, we got to know the family. We asked Chris about himself and what activities he liked to do outside of school. "That's a touchy topic right now," he answered, concerned. Clearly, we had struck a sensitive nerve, and his parents—whom we had met just moments before—launched into a tirade to explain that Chris attended a selective private school and had recently informed his parents that he no longer wanted to be a competitive diver. They went on to claim that he had been diving since he was three years old, traveled around the world, and had even competed on the United States Junior Diving Team. His parents recalled with great consternation how they had sacrificed everything for Chris's diving career, only to see him quit. How would he earn a coveted scholarship, and why on earth couldn't he at least wait until after diving for a year in college to make this decision? (All the while, I was quickly coming to the conclusion that his parents were failing miserably with their parenting skills!) Chris sat red-faced, uncomfortably wedged between them. He rebutted, "I'm tired of diving. I'm burnt out. It's all I have done since I was three years old. I want a break. I don't want to compete in college, and I just want to enjoy my senior year. And I have a plan: I'm going to fill my time with yearbook and other school-related activities."

Poor Chris. His parents didn't want to—couldn't—accept his decision, but Chris also reminded them (as we observed) that they were both working doctors and couldn't he also possibly attend a college without a diving scholarship? And that's when the conversation turned very *US-News-&-World-Report* focused. Chris's parents didn't want him to attend a "sub par" school. We finished lunch, and the conversation ended. We gave Chris a "be strong" fist bump and wished him luck.

Unfortunately, we don't know how the rest of Chris's high school or college experience turned out, but we surely felt that Chris's parents could benefit from practicing some lessons taught in *The Parent Compass*. Their behavior broke so many of the etiquette suggestions that this book tries to teach, and Chris's parents were not the kind of parents any kid would hope to have, publicly humiliating and berating him in front of absolute strangers. Perhaps too much togetherness had triggered this explosion, but Chris was a young adult who deserved to make his own choice and have his voice and opinion heard.

About Quinn

In contrast, Quinn's experience allows us to witness good parenting at work. A water polo player for most of her life, Quinn and her family had always assumed that her athletic skill coupled with her stellar grades would make her admissible to some of the most highly selective schools in the country—and she nearly was. But as her junior year came to a close, Quinn began to do some deep soul searching. One particular day, she sat across my desk from me in tears. A little background: From the moment I had met Quinn a couple years prior, both she and her parents emphatically characterized her as someone who naturally didn't express much emotion. She was deep in thought—always—but she wasn't especially emotive. But on this day, Quinn was inconsolable as she confessed to me that she wanted to quit water polo. At once, I heard the fear reflected behind her tears alongside the relief at having confessed this secret to someone. She played at an elite level, and she was aware that this decision would factor into her college process. As Quinn and I unpacked her thoughts, I learned of the incredible stress that had resulted from juggling her rigorous course load with her practices, tournaments, extra conditioning, and team commitments. While Quinn knew unequivocally that she no longer wanted to play water polo, no matter the impact it had on college admission, Quinn's biggest concern was disappointing her coach, her teammates, and her parents. But she agreed to let her parents in on her plan during the coming week: she was going to quit.

When I saw her a few weeks later, her unwavering desire to focus on the other areas of her life had remained unchanged, and she had had the courage to approach her parents. To her surprise, they had noticed the effect that water polo had on her emotional health. While they, too, understood that this would impact her college admission process, they decided to focus instead on supporting their daughter and her well-being. Quinn's parents saw how much their daughter had thought through this decision and recognized what a painful one it was to make. They heard her.

Quinn, now in college, went on to attend what her parents describe as the "best possible school for her." Quitting water polo meant uncovering new interests, and on any given week, Quinn can be found hurrying over to the university research lab that has sparked a deep desire in her to pursue medicine. Her parents use one happy word to describe her: "thriving."

Navigating Clubs with a Compass

Middle and high schools offer clubs in a variety of themes and levels of commitment. Some clubs meet weekly. Others monthly or even less. Some clubs meet at lunch, or before or after school. Others meet on the weekends or evenings. There are school-sponsored clubs, led by teachers, and there are student-directed ones. Some clubs are academic and require "homework" or project planning such as a debate or Model United Nations club, while others are purely social or common-interest themed such as a *Game of Thrones* or *Harry Potter* club. Whatever the case may be, if your teen joins a club, he should enjoy it, but he should also be able to discuss why he is in it and what he does with his time participating in meetings or club-sponsored events.

A particular club also can be invented or started by your teen if it doesn't exist at her school. For example, one of our students started a food-centered barbecue club where members met monthly, barbecued, and took turns planning the menu and sharing recipes. Another student founded her school's Scrabble Club since she liked to play the game competitively (with a chess clock and using two-letter words that are allowed in the Scrabble Dictionary). The club members attended tournaments, but they also welcomed members who preferred just to play socially.

As a parent, the same rules apply to your teen's club interests: support the clubs your teen decides to join. While the club choices should be made in light of his values and priorities, sometimes clubs can simply be for pleasure or for giving back to the community or learning something new. Don't encourage him to join a club just because you think it will "look good" for college. This is your teen's school experience, and he should be the one who chooses where and how he spends his ever-decreasing amount of free and recreational time. On the other hand, if your teen describes membership in a club as "boring" or a "waste of time," then by all means encourage him to join another instead, start one of his own, or spend his time productively elsewhere.

Navigating the Arts with a Compass

Whether playing a solo instrument or in a band or orchestra, participating in theater crew, tech, or as an actor, dancer, painter, photographer, sculptor, or singer (or any other form imaginable), the arts are an excellent outlet for your teen. The arts can also be therapeutic, relaxing, and soothing, as they open up and exercise other parts of your teen's brain in creative ways. Reading and writing music, interpreting dance moves, or blocking theater scenes can challenge a student's critical thinking and analytical skills. Parents, whether you think the arts are a worthwhile way to spend time or not, if your teen derives pleasure pursuing any of the arts, your job in practicing good behavior is to encourage, facilitate, and share in their interest—even if it is just by asking questions, attending performances and presentations, or playing chauffeur. And another bonus to exercising the right brain is that it fosters the "skills that will help promote and create a smarter and more productive adult better suited for the future workplace."[6]

Navigating Volunteerism with a Compass

About Yvonne

Yvonne was a high school freshman and a varsity basketball player when I met her. She shared with me that every Friday after school—when she didn't have basketball practice or a game—she shot hoops in her driveway, which was located on a neighborhood cul-de-sac. A few Fridays in a row she noticed some younger neighbors coming over to watch her practice. Her audience grew with each passing week. Word must have traveled around the playground and neighborhood. Sometimes the neighbor kids clapped when she scored a basket or held their breath when she attempted a layup. She often practiced free throws, and this small group of fans cheered and counted the number of baskets she could make in a row. Yvonne knew their names and sometimes allowed them to try some shots. The moms, dads, or babysitters would usually call the kids in for dinner or to wash up, and their time together would come to an end.

After a few weeks of pseudo-babysitting and coaching these pee-wees, a lightbulb went off for Yvonne. The following day, she went to her school community service advisor and proposed that she offer free basketball lessons to neighborhood kids. She posited that she could lead these informal clinics and help neighbor families while they prepared dinner or needed help with a child or two. The advisor directed her to write up a formal proposal and asked her to get the parents of the neighbor kids to agree to sign a card each time Yvonne held her clinic. And just like that, Yvonne formed her own community service opportunity, helping her neighbors occupy their kids for a scheduled chunk of time and teaching them some sports skills to go with it. The added bonus: Yvonne completed her community service hours easily and in a fun way, and she even continued her program into some summer weeks, enlisting the help of a few of her teammates.

If your teen's middle or high school has an annual community service requirement, sure, she needs to do it. But really, the most valuable service experiences are those that serve others *and* are fulfilling, springing from a student's related interest (like Yvonne's love for basketball) and identifying a need in the community. Consider encouraging your teen to go beyond simply amassing a certain number of hours just to meet a requirement and come up with a service opportunity that truly means something to her.

The Corporation for National and Community Service published these statistics about youth volunteerism:[7]

- Approximately 15.5 million youth—or 55 percent of youth ages twelve to eighteen—participate in volunteer activities.

- Youth contribute more than 1.3 billion hours of community service annually.

- Youth volunteer an average of twenty-nine hours per year.

- Thirty-nine percent of teen volunteers are "regular" volunteers who volunteer at least twelve weeks per year.

Many parents also participate in community service with their teens in organizations such as National Charity League (NCL) or National League of Young Men (NLYM). While sharing service experiences with your teen can be a significant bonding experience, it is even more important that your teen find something that he enjoys doing *on his own*. In fact, while NCL and NLYM are certainly worthwhile organizations, why not consider foregoing the joint community service experience to guide your teen into finding an experience that he enjoys doing solo?

Some inspiring ideas and places for teens to start volunteering are:

- Tutoring at a local Boys & Girls Club, church, or after-school assistance program

- Teaching an instrument, dance, or the arts to underserved youngsters

- Donating time to a local nature sanctuary or farm

- Cleaning horse stables, camp sites, beaches, or local parks

- Serving meals at a soup kitchen or homeless shelter

- Volunteering at a local public library or community center

- Packing boxes at nearby food banks

- Organizing a school or neighborhood collection of items to be donated, whether used sports equipment, books, school supplies, personal hygiene items, or clothing for those in need

- Volunteering for Special Olympics, local fundraiser races, or your church

- Creating or coordinating a class or workshop to teach others about an interest or a niche specialty

Some of these volunteer activities can also be performed online, so consider reaching out to organizations that need virtual volunteer assistance or propose your own. But remember: the key for your teen is to volunteer *and* enjoy it.

Navigating Teen Jobs with a Compass

How many of you somewhat mindlessly hand your kids cash, a credit card, or Apple Pay on a Friday night to fund pizza with friends or a trip to the shopping mall? What would happen if, instead, your kids earned their own money to pay for these indulgences on their own? Encouraging your teen to work in order to earn spending or gas money is not a punishment; it is a life lesson and good parenting. Doling out cash is enabling, and encouraging work to earn one's own money is just the opposite.

Indeed, it is a sad reality that not nearly enough of our students have held down a job before they graduate from high school. Interestingly enough, though, the maturity, responsibility, and lessons learned by the ones who have tend to set them apart from their peers. Some parents tell us that they don't want their teens to work, citing that it can hurt their grades in school. But we encourage you to think more creatively;

getting a job doesn't have to happen during the school week, unless your teen has the time to add work to her schedule or if work is a necessary family priority. Teens can also schedule work on the weekends, in the summers, on school breaks, or even virtually, and in turn, they will learn to balance a part-time job with their other activities.

Here are some appropriate jobs for teens:

- Babysitting

- Bagging groceries

- Scooping ice cream

- Walking dogs

- Mowing lawns

- Getting a neighbor's mail, watering plants, or rolling in trash cans while they travel

- Helping in an office

- Doing household chores

- Running a neighborhood summer camp (craft, sports, games, cheer, cooking, academic, etc.)

- Working for a Jewish Community Center, YMCA, Boys & Girls Club, or any camp as a teen counselor or counselor in training

- Working at a retail store (folding clothes, restocking, cashier)

- Hosting or bussing at a local restaurant

- Getting a job at a business that does something your teen is excited about (e.g., a photography studio if your teen is into photography)

- Working virtually as a tutor, dance teacher, paid intern, web designer, singing or music instructor, or social media consultant

A part-time job leads to valuable life lessons such as how to apply for a job, interview skills, people skills, showing up on time, taking responsibility for actions, and learning the real value of a dollar, among other things. So, the next time your teen asks you for money to go shopping, kindly use your best parenting skills and suggest that he find a way to earn and spend his own money. And then when he purchases an article of clothing or agrees to a pizza night out, he can quantify the purchase with the number of hours of work it took him to earn it.

About Sonia

When Sonia was in middle school, she and her two younger siblings really wanted to get a Ping-Pong table that they had seen on display at a local sporting goods store, but it was expensive. Envisioning family game nights and friendly after-school battles, Sonia and her siblings approached their parents, who wisely made their kids a deal: if Sonia and her siblings could work together to earn half of the money for it, they would match the earnings and pay for the other half. "But how can we earn that kind of money when we are just kids?" Sonia pointed out. And then the brainstorming began: lemonade stands; dog walking; odd jobs around the house; and offering to wash cars, roll out trash cans, get mail, or water plants while neighbors were away. Sonia and her siblings went to work. They even cleaned out their closets and organized a garage sale under their mom's supervision. They collected cans and plastic water bottles from their home, neighbors, and at nearby youth sports fields and brought them in to their grocery store to collect money from recycling. The kids put out a plastic beach bucket on the kitchen counter as a collection spot for every coin and dollar bill that they had earned. By the end of the summer, Sonia and her siblings had miraculously reached their goal. Their parents upheld their end of the bargain, too, and with great pride, the new Ping-Pong table was purchased. When friends came over to use it, Sonia chided them to be careful not to drag their paddles or scratch it. The value of hard work to earn a reward was instilled in Sonia and her siblings at a young age, and this lesson has stayed with her. Sonia shared this story with me with such enthusiasm and joy, recalling the feeling of earning money and positive teamwork with her siblings. What she also described to me was great parenting in practice.

About Justin and Jacob

Many years ago, when my (now college-age) sons Justin and Jacob were in middle school, they co-founded and created a neighborhood *Star Wars* Summer Camp. The boys told me that they wanted to make money in the summer and have a "real" job, so they came up with an idea—a camp that they wished they could have had when they were younger. The first summer they enrolled about ten campers between the ages of five and ten years old. At camp, the kids played school-yard games that Justin and Jacob had invented and modified: "Red Lightsaber/Green Lightsaber," "What time is it, Darth Vader?," and "Luke, Luke, Leia" (Duck, Duck, Goose). Campers "visited" *Star Wars* planets, which were in the form of small printed signs taped onto trees around the park. While at the planets, Justin, Jacob, and the campers discussed what happened on each one, who lived there, who fought there, and who won. The campers built *Star Wars* ships and inventions out of our loaned buckets of LEGO, filled in *Star Wars* coloring books and crossword puzzles, ate *Star Wars* gummy candies at snack time, and watched *Star Wars* movie clips on a laptop. The week ended with a *Star Wars* costume parade where campers dressed in everything from Obi-Wan Kenobi robes to Jango Fett masks to *Star Wars* pajamas and marched around the park to the tunes of the *Star Wars* movie soundtrack. I gently supervised at camp sign-in and sign-out and as the adult on-site chaperone in case any emergencies arose, but Justin and Jacob were fully in charge of running all of the activities and problem-solving as situations emerged. This was *their* job, not mine. As the years progressed and the summer camp grew, they even employed their younger siblings (who began as campers) to be Jedi Youngling "helpers." By their fifth summer, the camp had sold out and tripled its enrollment; they even added an afternoon *Star Wars* Movie Camp where the films were screened, stopped, paused, discussed, and analyzed. Justin and Jacob had created a very popular and fun camp and a quite lucrative job for themselves.

The *Star Wars* Camp ran for several summers until the boys graduated and left for college. Taking an interest, creating a business out of thin air, and building this program was an achievement that both of them cherished and enjoyed. They were stimulated, and they were exhausted; they were proud of what they accomplished and of the campers that they had inspired. Half of Justin and Jacob's earnings went into savings and the other half into a LEGO *Star Wars* purchase to which they treated themselves for a job well done. Life lessons, problem-solving, entrepreneurship, and personal pride were all skills that the boys gained through this rewarding and creative experience. And I tried hard to be well-intentioned and follow my compass rather than be a hands-on facilitator of their program.

Q: Is it better to participate in a lot of activities and have less involvement or partake in a few activities with a deeper commitment?

A: *There is no right or wrong way to answer this question. Many colleges appreciate pointy students—those with a deep interest in one or two activities that permeate their extracurricular focus—but they also appreciate students who are well-rounded and are involved in a variety of activities. Colleges appreciate students with both depth and breadth. The best answer to this question would be to see what your teen enjoys doing coupled with how much she can handle while doing well in school. If activities add too much stress, take up too much time, and impact how your teen is performing in the classroom, then it is worth examining and refining the activity list to try to find the best point of balance. Some students thrive from having a lot of balls in the air and multi-tasking while others need to keep things evenly balanced to maintain their grades and their sanity. There is no right or wrong way to do this.*

Finding Balance

We would be remiss to neglect the topic of balance and downtime here, which we discuss more in depth in Chapter 5. But, you might wonder, is recreation even possible in the crazy busy world in which we live? And to that question, we emphatically answer, "Yes!" Recreation comes in all shapes and sizes. It is what helps us refill our tank; it is what we look forward to when a long project comes to a close or final examinations are finished. It is the reward for a day, week, or month spent working hard.

Downtime is important for every teen no matter how they choose to spend it. Whether it is meditating, tackling a Rubik's Cube, binge-watching a show, going for a walk, challenging friends to a board game, visiting the beach, or taking a long drive while belting out a favorite song with the windows down, it just doesn't matter. When built into your teen's life, recreation adds breathing room into a hyper-connected and competitive academic landscape. Want to pull your kid out of school for a day for an unexpected trip to the beach or local amusement park—or maybe for a day of quiet and connection? We respond with a resounding yes (as long as it's not too often).

CHAPTER 5:

NAVIGATE LIFE AFTER 3:00 PM

Alex panicked as he furiously worked the mathematical puzzle before him. Acutely aware of time ticking behind him, he groaned as he realized he might actually let his family down this time. Nearby, his sister nervously shouted out suggestions, her voice high pitched as she, too, felt the pressure of the moment. With her help, Alex solved the complicated problem, then gathered another clue that would help free his family from this claustrophobic nightmare, and, together, he and his mom decoded its meaning. With that one out of the way, the family discovered an ornate key, but which door did it operate? Did it even operate a door? With seconds to spare, Alex's father slid the key into the correct lock, and the family burst through the exit door. This was an ordinary Saturday night for Alex's family.

Escape room fanatics, Alex and his family routinely travel near and far for their monthly escape room outing, hungry to keep experiencing the collaborative nature of the activity and the problem-solving skills that it engenders in each family member. The family works together to solve puzzle after puzzle, problem after problem, to escape the room in which they have been locked. Mom, Dad, Alex, and his sister each have a valuable voice as they work together toward the common goal of freedom. Not surprisingly, Alex's family is extremely close-knit. Family time in their home is exciting, challenging, and collaborative, and every member feels seen and heard.

Parents, your appropriate support of your teen's life outside of the classroom, including family time, plays just as important of a role in his development, well-being, and positive view of the world as does your support of his purely academic life. In this chapter, we will focus on parent compass rules for family time and downtime, supporting your student when the school day is done, and determining if you should hire extra help for your child.

Playtime, Downtime, and Family Time

Challenge Success is an important nonprofit research and intervention program that partners with schools, communities, and families, and it is changing our academic landscape by challenging our conceptualization of "success." One of the strategies that Challenge Success suggests to promote good teen health and well-being is the importance of daily playtime, downtime, and family time, or "PDF," for optimal development. Students—whether youngsters, teens, or even college age—need time during each day to step away from their otherwise over-scheduled existence and do something just for fun—to play. What's more, they say, "research shows that when kids are part of a family unit that spends time together, they are likely to feel supported, safe, and loved unconditionally as well as have increased self-esteem and better academic outcomes."[1] Taking that one step further, creating parental one-on-one time with each individual child in a family, whether it be playing a game or embarking on an outing, can be hugely beneficial and can allow a special connection to develop that isn't distracted by other sibling or parental dynamics. Maybe you and your teen share a deep appreciation for an old-fashioned root beer float. Make a bi-weekly date to indulge without the distraction of siblings or significant others. Maybe your tween can't get enough of musicals. Plan a monthly outing to check out free, low-cost, or local school performances together. If you are intentional about marking it on your calendars, you will be more likely to prioritize this restorative time together.

Likewise, it's strange to think that downtime needs to be scheduled; it would seem that it can be achieved organically, but if you are actively following your parent compass, you should be scheduling it. As adults, we do feel the beneficial effects of self-care; some of us practice it better than others, but we can all agree that a warm bubble bath or long, hot shower, time spent engrossed in a good book, a mind-clearing run, or a well-deserved vacation inevitably lifts our spirits. Similarly, downtime helps our teens to relax, reset, and recharge from the overly programmed and very active life that usually consumes them. Whether it comes in the form of a nap, meditation, or listening to music, help your teen fine-tune her practice of regular downtime; you will be providing her with an invaluable gift.

Ensure Enough Sleep

Getting enough sleep is so crucial for you and your teen—indeed entire books have been written on the subject. A robust body of research shows that not sleeping enough hours comes at a huge cost for our kids, resulting in many negative consequences in personal safety, learning in school, physical health, and even emotional stability. By now you've probably heard that the use of technology before bedtime can significantly impact sleep. Indeed, the light given off by screens alters sleep patterns and depth of sleep, but do you really enforce rules around this indisputable fact? We resolutely recommend helping your teen shut down all devices for a full hour before he goes to bed. Collecting cell phones, iPads, and laptops is a necessary nightly habit (see Chapter 6 for a more in-depth discussion of technology in the home).

As you practice, become familiar with these important sleep statistics. Share this research with your kids if they resist your encouragement to choose more sleep:

"Surveys show that many teenagers do not get the recommended nine hours sleep a night and report having trouble staying awake at school."

"Teenagers who go to bed late during the school year are more prone to academic and emotional difficulties in the long run, compared to teens [who are] in bed earlier, according to a new study from University of California, Berkeley."[2]

About Leticia

Leticia seemed to me to be the typical American teenager; she was busy with school, extracurricular activities, and an active social life both personal and through social media. And not surprisingly, like a typical American teenager, Leticia also appeared exhausted when I met with her—disheveled, dark circles under her eyes, and dozing off every now and then. But when I asked her how much time it took for her to complete her homework each night, she replied, "About six hours." "And about how much sleep do you get?" I followed up. "About five hours," she replied. "Are you tired?" I guess I didn't even need to ask. She nodded as tears filled her eyes. When we took the time to break down the hours she spent on homework and analyze the location of her social media devices and her study space, it turned out that several of these basic setups were somehow just off. Leticia habitually grabbed a candy bar from her school vending machine after school before heading to her sports team practice. She returned to an empty home around 6:00 PM since both parents worked late or were carpooling her younger sibling. A healthy meal wasn't usually on hand, so after she showered, she scraped up something for dinner. By 7:00 PM she could start her homework, which she did on her big comfy bed with a backrest of pillows; but before starting her work, Leticia caught up on social networking and texts, which usually took about thirty minutes. Homework began at approximately 7:30 PM and included a nearby cell phone, the buzz and beep of messages and notifications constantly interrupting her. She began with her easiest and favorite subjects first, and homework usually lasted until around 1:30 AM. Sometimes, about once a week, Leticia woke up in the night with papers around her, the laptop almost out of battery, and the bedroom light still on. Leticia was up again at 6:00 AM to shower and start all over again, as she had a zero-period class. Sound familiar?

It came as no surprise that it was difficult for Leticia to keep up this pace, which was taking its toll on her sleep and mental health. So together, we mapped out a weekly plan, dividing up her time into thirty-minute chunks and asking her mom to assist with having meals ready to heat up (or at minimum frozen dinners) on the nights her mom worked late. Leticia disciplined herself to limit her social media intake (in order to gain sleep time by decreasing homework time), left her phone down in the kitchen while she studied, and installed an app that turned off her computer messaging as well. She relocated her study location from her bed to her desk (which was previously covered in clothes!) and began a system of doing homework in thirty-minute increments. Every thirty minutes, Leticia could take a break for about five minutes: stand up and stretch or use the restroom, grab a snack, or play with her dog. Then it was back to another thirty-minute increment. After each hour, Leticia could check and respond to five minutes of social media messages. And what do you know? Leticia's time spent on nightly homework decreased from six hours to three hours, and her sleep time increased to eight or nine hours. With her new plan implemented—and knowing that this discipline is not always sustainable during exam season or when big projects are due—Leticia wielded some structure and control over her time, instead of letting a broken and failing system overtake her. Leticia's system is just one example of how your teen can implement a plan to increase sleep time, and as a parent, reading this story should alert you to things you can do to help your own child should he show signs of exhaustion like Leticia did.

Eat Family Meals Together

Seemingly a Herculean task with teens' competing schedules, work, and after-school commitments, family meals have a vastly positive impact on family dynamics and on general well-being. Studies show that these gatherings greatly improve mental health, and by extension, result in better sleep and happiness in school. According to the *Journal of Youth & Adolescence*, "Adolescents who frequently ate meals with their family and/ or parents were less likely to engage in risk behaviors when compared to peers who never or rarely ate meals with their families."[3] Parents, it is never too late to start this ritual. Choose at least one evening per week—or as many as you humanly can; research says that five to seven nights is optimal—to sit down together for a meal.[4] "A moody teen who refuses to talk is a common pop-culture cliché. But scientific surveys of thousands of teens paint a different picture. Most teens actually value their relationships with their parents and want to spend time with them. This is also true at dinner. About eighty percent of teenagers report that they'd rather have dinner with their families than by themselves or with friends. And when adolescents are asked to list their favorite activities, family dinner ranks high on that list."[5]

Some families schedule the (often) impossible-to-achieve family dinner on Friday or Sunday evenings, deeming it a non-optional, non-negotiable family commitment. If one parent works non-traditional hours or travels often, sharing these dinners with one parent or even with an extended family member can accomplish the same goal.[6] Impress upon your complainers and eye rollers that this is not a punishment but a family tradition that needs to be upheld for everyone to bond and, just as importantly, for emotional well-being. It doesn't matter if you order in, take out, or whip up a special recipe, gathering around a table to break bread for breakfast, lunch, or dinner is one of the best activities you can help facilitate for your family. If you are able to involve your kids—especially on the weekends, when they may not have as much homework or enjoy a little bit more free time—then all the better. Grocery shop with them or send them to the grocery store with a list, food prep and cook with them, or have them set the table and help with cleanup—all of this togetherness in contributing to a family gathering promotes mental health and positivity. And it allows for loose, unstructured conversation and laughter.

In fact, in our homes we leave a boxed game on the dinner table called Table Topics, which gets everyone to weigh in on their views and gives each member a valued voice. Family ice breakers also take the focus away from discussion surrounding schoolwork and grades and instead lend to more creative thinking and authentic sharing. Family debates, discoveries of different perspectives, uncontrollable laughter, and surprising insights have resulted from that powerful little box. (For some hands-on ideas, see note 7.)

A White Paper produced by Columbia University's National Center on Addiction and Substance Abuse makes the case for family dinners.

- Teens who have frequent family dinners (at least five per week) are 1.5 times more likely to say that their parents know a great deal/fair amount about what's really going on in their lives than teens who have infrequent family dinners (less than three family dinners per week).

- Those who say their parents know very little/nothing at all about what goes on in their lives are 1.5 times more likely to have used marijuana and alcohol.

- Teens who have frequent family meals report having high-quality relationships with their parents. These teens are less likely to use drugs, drink, or smoke.

- Teens who have frequent family meals are 1.5 times less likely to report high levels of stress and, thus, less likely to have used marijuana, alcohol, or tobacco.

- Teens who have infrequent family meals are less likely to say their parents would be extremely upset to find they had used marijuana and are three times more likely to say that their parents do not disapprove of marijuana or alcohol use.[8]

Establishing a Family Calendar

While navigating your parent compass, it is important that you have some general understanding of your teen's after-school and academic schedule. While your role is not to micromanage these time blocks, you should be generally familiar with what their days look like: Are there late-start days? Is there time after school and before sports to get any work done, eat, or even rest a bit? Sure, schedules are always in flux, but it never hurts to check in and see if you can be of assistance with small, supportive tasks.

But perhaps more importantly, your teen should also have all of her commitments scheduled somewhere for herself. Remember: supporting your teen in establishing *her* self-sufficiency should be one of your main parenting goals. In fact, as you refine your personal goals, we implore you to prod your teen to maintain her *own* calendar—the easiest might be an electronic calendar app such as a Yahoo, Gmail, or iCal calendar—with her important dates and deadlines, doctor's appointments, practices, and games. It is surprising and disappointing to us as professionals who work with teens how many of our students are simply unable to schedule their own appointments. They don't keep their own calendars and instead rely on their parents to plan out their days. Parents, if your high school student is unable to schedule meetings, appointments, and other important activities on her own, you are not practicing good parenting; she is virtually tethered to you. Instead, your teen should get in the habit of using a calendar to map out her meetings, activities, and even long-term commitments or projects that are required in each of her classes: an end-of-the year presentation? A PowerPoint project? Something that requires special school supplies like poster board, glue, or stick-on letters? Encourage your teen to manage her own calendar.

Building upon this practice, the best way to know where everyone in your family is while enabling a sense of independence and self-sufficiency is to maintain a centralized family calendar—whether it is written decoratively on a whiteboard on display in the kitchen, hallway, or garage, or better yet quickly and easily accessed on an electronic online calendar that all family members can sync, access, and update on demand. (Hundreds of great ideas for family calendars are posted on Pinterest or online to get you started if you have not already.) E-calendars allow you to import daily, weekly, or monthly repeating events and also allow you to color code. We suggest color coding each person in your family so that you can see who is where and when. And changes to these e-calendars can be made from a cell phone, iPad, or computer—so they can be updated and synced in real time. Doctor and dentist appointments, sports games, and family events should all be able to be seen and accessed immediately, removing the constant need for your teen to check with you before planning something. As a result, your teen will learn self-reliance and responsibility, and he will be decreasingly dependent on you when it comes time to schedule something new.

Supporting Your Teen When the School Day Is Over

"Don't tell me what to do," might be a comment we hear from our teens from time to time (alongside a furrowed brow and unwavering tone of voice). To that comment we can agree, but we are still their guides and consultants. Let your high school child know that you are not interested in managing her life—that you know it is not your job anymore. Instead you want to support her in any way she needs you to, whether it is giving her rides, helping to arrange carpools, or teaching her how to tune up her bike or change a tire. Notice that we said "teaching her how to tune up her bike." Fellow parents, be careful you don't enable or take over; just be supportive if asked. If your teen is in middle school, keep in mind that some kids are ready before others for their parents to back off, while others still really want your help, input, and participation.

Stock the Fridge

Let's face it, most teens arrive home from school ravenous. When my own kids get home from school, they head straight for the refrigerator and pantry. Keep a running grocery list of healthy foods that your child would like you to stock. Too much sugar eventually results in fatigue, and a tired brain does not yield a productive studier. Salty, sugary carbs may cause your teen to get sleepy while doing homework, as their body is busy digesting these sugars. Try to have fresh fruits and veggies with yogurt or ranch dressing on hand (or other healthy alternatives) to dunk them into. Often, watermelon slices, bunches of grapes (fresh or frozen), and other easy, healthy choices can be ready to grab and go. Whether you are a parent who carpools, works outside of the home, or greets your kids at the front door, it doesn't matter as long as there are good choices for your teen to heat up or pull from a container.

Help to Create a Useful Study Space

If your child has gotten into the bad habit of doing homework in a soft, comfortable bed or on a plush, fluffy couch, or if your teen prefers to do homework at the kitchen table, help him to change those bad habits. Invest in a desk where he can spread out in a quiet, well-lit area such as a bedroom or study. The location should be free from unnecessary distractions such as a television, noisy younger siblings, or family members shuffling in and out. Be sure the desk has not only a ceiling light shining down on it but also a desk lamp. Pick out a chair that your teen likes, maybe an office chair with wheels or a sturdy wooden chair that is not too comfortable. Provide basic supplies: a stapler, tape, paper clips, loose-leaf paper, Post-it notes, notepads, mechanical pencils and pens, highlighters, and even a filing system that your teen likes to use. If a personal laptop fits into your budget, then provide one for your teen—it doesn't have to be an expensive one. Some schools also provide computers or iPads to certain classes or to students who have financial need.

Other helpful, inspiring study tips:

- Encourage your teen to turn off her cell phone or leave it outside of the study area while getting schoolwork done. Try putting a common phone docking station near your front or back door or in the kitchen; this is a good way to keep family cell phones charged and also unglued from each person.

- Suggest that your teen start with the homework from his hardest class and/or the subject he likes the least. You can also incentivize him to do that work while he is freshest, rather than saving it for the end of the night when he may be tired and out of steam.

- Offer to set a timer for her. Working in timed increments also helps, so ask your teen if you can help in any way to make homework more bearable, doable, and efficient for her.

"Nearly one in three (31 percent) 8- to 18-year-olds say that 'most' of the time they are doing homework, they are also using one medium or another—watching TV, texting, listening to music, and so on."[9]

Staffing Up (Or Not): Navigating Tutors, Coaches, Therapists, and Consultants

Parents, when did tutoring become an extracurricular activity? Does it seem like everyone around you is hiring extra help for their kids? Even in subjects in which the kids are doing well? Why is it that our society has become so "tutor dependent"? Is it because parents are fearful that their kids will fail and by extension not get into an "acceptable" college?

Just as we encourage our kids to not succumb to peer pressure, so, too, must *we* resist parental pressure. The cocktail party dialogues, sideline chats, and parenting gossip have gotten out of control. We know that parents can feel pressure to "keep up with the Joneses." Comparing yourself and your parenting choices with other toxic parents increases your own personal level of anxiety with regard to your teen; *comparing takes away joy and creates tension.* This is never a good thing—especially because the stress we feel trickles down to our kids. Do not fall prey to these tiger parents (but *do* loan them a copy of this book!). Frankly, the overbearing parents—and we know who they are and how they behave—can mess with your personal sanity. Breathe, follow your parent compass, and know that by doing so you are doing right by your teen.

Some families consider tutors a necessity for their teens. In fact, in a recent Challenge Success survey, 64.8 percent of parents of high school students reported that they had hired paid tutors for their children during high school. Interestingly, 36 percent of parents surveyed said that they checked their kids' grades weekly, while 11 percent reported that they went so far as to check them daily.[10]

Encourage your teen to use school support services including the teacher, peer tutors, or tutorial periods first before resorting to a paid tutor. Recognizing when your teen needs more help than a teacher or you can offer is an important function that you can provide. Many parents make the mistake of hiring a multitude of tutors to oversee homework and help in more classes than their teen needs. This practice is a mistake. *Relying on tutors makes teens dependent on them and, as a result, less self-sufficient.*

Tutoring Concerns

One small Bay Area town has ten tutoring centers within a four-block radius—*ten!* At 3:00 PM each day, students pour out from the seven nearby public and private middle and high schools and parade into these centers, filling up tutor spots with eagerly paying customers. Let us ask again: *When did tutoring become an extracurricular activity?* And is there no shame or concern about hundreds of kids from both private and public schools attending these sessions multiple times per week? We have even considered conducting an informal, local social experiment and some investigative reporting. In this experiment, we would ask random middle and high school students who were entering and exiting tutoring centers the following questions:

1. How many times per week do you attend a tutoring center (or have an at-home private tutor)?

2. In how many subjects do you get assistance?

3. Do you feel the tutoring has helped you do better in school?

4. Do your tutors help you more than your school teachers?

5. Do you like attending tutoring sessions?

6. Whose idea was it to get a tutor?

7. For how many years have you seen tutors?

8. Does your school have a study skills center, teacher office hours, or tutorials?

9. Do you feel academic stress at school, and if so, does a tutor help you manage that?

10. Do your tutors ever do your homework for you, write papers, or "overstep" their roles by telling you answers or completing assignments for you?

We imagine that we would be shocked at the replies. It is our educated hunch—and many a helicopter and tiger parent has shared in confidence their awful honest truths about how they would answer these questions—that most students would reveal that the tutors themselves completed homework for them or wrote the actual words that they submitted in their school assignments. Other students might complain that this tutoring was a waste of time and money, but that their parents made them go to tutors since "everyone else was." Those who went to centers might even share that they also had additional at-home tutors.

And then there is a very concerning new breed of tutoring center that has emerged in a Chicago suburb. This is not the run-of-the-mill tutoring space with desks and one-on-one or group sessions. This is instead a membership-driven "tutoring lounge." Yes, you read that right: *a tutoring lounge*. What is a tutoring lounge, you ask? It's a hang-out space adorned with cool, hip decor, where music serenades its student-clients who enjoy unbridled access to one-on-one and group tutoring spaces. The cost to be a member is $250 per month . . . oh, and no parents are allowed beyond the entry area. Very short five- to ten-minute tutoring sessions are included, but at the touch of a phone app button, students can book half-hour sessions for special needs that they may have. And in the big business of tutoring, with some estimates putting its value at $227 billion by 2022, we fear that this trendy hangout/tutoring center may catch on and blossom in more suburban communities.[11] Joining one of these membership-driven tutoring centers seems over the top to us and is evidence of poor or lazy parenting—through and through.

About Robin

During a recent tour of an acquaintance's new home, we approached a carefully curated room. Beaming, Robin proudly showed off to me her "tutoring room." Without a hint of embarrassment, she remarked, "The three kids have so many tutors coming over at various times after school that we decided to create a workspace for them all." The space included reference books, computer monitors, and even Cliff's Notes and study guides in almost every subject at a variety of grade levels. Observing this space, I felt like I was in the reference aisle of Barnes & Noble. My first thought was, "Why on earth would her kids need so many tutors, and have they exhausted the use of their school teachers and peer support?" But most concerning: How would these students ever learn to do things on their own when they go to college? Tutoring should be used in moderation and as needed and should be curbed as comprehension and grades improve. *The goal should not be to overload on tutors.* This dedicated space was clearly an exhibit of an overreaching, overzealous, over-panicked parent.

When to Hire a Tutor

So, when should you hire a tutor? It is our opinion, and that of many school teachers and administrators, that there is a natural order for seeking professional academic help. When all else fails, if your teen is frustrated and not getting support from his teacher or a peer tutor, is befuddled and overwhelmed, or is struggling in a class then it is probably time to seek professional help. A good rule of thumb? Earning a C grade or below could necessitate enlisting the help of a weekly tutor. Your teen should have always met with the teacher a few times *before* you hire a tutor in a subject.

And don't have the tutor come more than once per week to start so that your teen isn't dependent on doing all of her homework with a tutor.

Here is our recommended order of events to determine when to hire a tutor:

1. Has your child already gone directly to his teacher for help or office hours?

2. Has your child attended school tutorials and/or visited the school's study skills center (if there is one)?

3. Has your teen sought out upperclassmen who have taken the course or a classmate who is doing very well in the course to turn to for help?

4. Has your teen visited Khan Academy, YouTube or other online academic support services that teach thousands of classes and concepts?

5. Has your teen asked you or an older sibling for help? And, is this a subject in which you can offer some assistance?

Hiring a tutor should be a last resort decision. Once all of the above are pursued and exhausted, then it is probably time to hire a tutor for supplemental help. Commit to one day a week first and move up only as needed. Plan to wean off of a tutor once your teen has progressed through the hard period in that class—until eventually, there is no need for a tutor.

A tutor should not be a crutch on which a student becomes dependent to get through his classes. Having too many tutors creates lazier, dependent students who are less likely to self-advocate and is clear evidence of poor and lazy parenting. Schools offer plenty of resources on campus—namely the teacher first and oftentimes an on-campus study skills center staffed with older peers or teachers in a variety of subjects—that are usually free. It is up to your teen to take advantage of these offerings first. Review sessions, office hours, and tutorial sessions should be noted on your teen's calendars, too, as if these time periods are simply an extended offering on top of the actual courses. As a curious parent, ask your teen what steps he usually takes when he needs help in a subject.

When to Hire a Therapist

If you are not able to talk through your concerns and help your teen with deeper issues, find someone who can help her. Some common red flags are if your child is exhibiting signs of depression, experiencing excessive weight gain or loss, struggling in school, or expressing a concerning level of anxiety. These may be signs that your teen needs professional help. School counselors are often available on campus and are a good place to start. If your teen needs more professional help, find a great therapist who specializes in adolescent issues. Having an unbiased person in your teen's life that she can talk to uninhibited and in a safe, confidential environment is one of the best supportive actions that you can provide to your child. Fellow parents, be proactive. There is no shame in seeking help; rather there could be even greater damage inflicted on your teen by ignoring her faltering emotional health. (Many employee health insurance plans offer fully covered in-network—and sometimes free—mental health care with face-to-face therapists as well as therapists online or by phone through organizations such as Lyra. Check out what your plan offers.)

When to Reach Out to Coaches

Athletic coaches, theater directors, dance instructors, religious group leaders, or club teacher liaisons can also be excellent trusted supports for your teen. These adults witness your teen in environments that are not academic, and they can often forge deeper relationships with your teen. Sometimes these coaches serve as their teachers too, thereby knowing your child in another capacity. Encourage your teen to seek out these mentors if issues arise that they want help navigating or if they just want a second opinion on a situation occurring in their life.

When to Hire an Educational Consultant

Finally, educational consultants—also known as private college counselors—can serve a helpful role in your child's teenage years. These consultants—like us—are paid professionals who help teens navigate middle and high school and ultimately the college application process. Many educational consultants have a psychology background, but even if they don't, they can be an extra set of eyes and ears on your teen. Students share a lot with private consultants, too, about their parents, school situations, interests, hopes, and worries. Hiring a private counselor, however, is like hiring a tutor; it is not necessary. While the college admission process can be daunting and overwhelming, many teens are able to stay on task and meet deadlines, and choose to work exclusively with their school counselor while seeking help from older siblings or students who have been through the process. Some even seek out the help of a high school English teacher.

Parents, don't feel pressured to hire a private counselor, but if you do, be sure that your teen enjoys working with him or her since they will be spending many hours in this process together. Be certain that the counselor you hire is current with college application and admission requirements; has experience as a former school counselor, is a former college admission office staff member, or has gained certification from a program in college counseling; stays abreast of college campus trends; and attends conferences or continuing education with the Independent Educational Consultants Association (IECA), Higher Education Consultants Association (HECA), or the National Association for College Admission Counseling (NACAC) or its regional affiliates. Of course, be wary of private counselors who guarantee that they can get your son or daughter into a particular college. This is not only a big red flag but also impossible to do (legally!), even if your teen has a strong legacy or is a recruited athlete. In contrast, the only guarantee a college counselor should ever give to you was beautifully coined by one of our veteran colleagues: "If you don't apply, you won't get in."

Build Your Village (Avoid Parental Peer Pressure and Help One Another Instead)

Finally, we need to turn the clock back to the days of sharing helpful information on the benches at the playground, allowing ourselves to be vulnerable so that we can build parent connections, and creating a village of supportive adults who can share the ups and downs of child rearing together. We need to compare less and judge less. We'll say it again: *comparing takes away joy*. Being vulnerable, on the other hand, builds connection. Parents, we need to stop judging, gossiping, assuming, and labeling.

A poignant *Grown and Flown* article eloquently cited many of the problems that parents are stirring up today when they pass judgment on others. We encourage you to read the essay, "It's Easy to Judge until It's Your Kid, Let's Try Compassion," by Marybeth Bock. The author makes many useful points, reminding us not to judge other people's kids, for eventually those judgments may be about our own kids. Here are a few highlights directly quoted from her piece:

- "Oh, how we are quick to judge. As parents of teens and young adults, we may find ourselves judging other people's kids as a means to teach or guide our own. Or to tear down and gossip about other kids in a misguided attempt to make our own seem superior in some way."

- "It's easy to think the know-it-all, overachiever kid is obnoxious and tries way too hard. Until it's your kid and you know they are on the spectrum and struggle daily with fully grasping social cues."

- "It's easy to blame the mean girls because your daughter was excluded from a birthday celebration and is so sad. Until you discover it was your child who also treated others with disrespect or insensitivity."

- "We are quick to judge. We are quick to joke. We are quick to accept rumors. And to label and to make assumptions. *And we need to stop.*"

- "Our kids are listening, even when we think they are not paying attention . . . [and] each new day presents us with a new opportunity to share in our humanity, extend grace, and practice compassion."[12]

We are a village. It's pretty plain and simple. An anonymous quote posted many times around the Internet reminds us that we need this fundamental support—to help one another and look out for each other's kids in productive, helpful, non-competitive ways. Consider sharing this with a friend via text or posting on your own social media:

Dear Fellow Parents of Teens,

If you see something my kid is doing that's dangerous, say something. It may be awkward and not well received at first, but it can make a difference: it could save a life. If you have knowledge about dangerous behavior going around school, I want to know. If you are aware of something that could affect the well-being of my child, I want to know. If my kid is the one being dangerous, I want to know. Send me a text or email, leave a note on my car, or do the unthinkable and pick up the phone. But, parents of older kids, please stay in my village. It's a scary world out there and we need each other.

CHAPTER 6:

TACKLE TECHNOLOGY WITH INTENTION, NOT IN TENSION

Just the other evening around 9:00 PM, I was multitasking on my computer—writing, paying bills, perusing Facebook, and allowing myself to be lured into the vortex of the World Wide Web by streaming videos, reading news articles, responding to texts, and clicking around on ads for items that the Internet seemingly magically picked just for me (thanks, cookies!). I had spent some money on Amazon, written part of a chapter for this book, and drafted two incomplete emails. Sound familiar? This is a typical evening activity in my home, usually timed after school-activity carpooling (a.k.a. mom taxiing) and dinner, but before I head upstairs to check in with my spouse, watch a few shows, quickly catch up on our daily lives, and go to bed. My two older sons are in college, and my two teenagers at home are very self-sufficient. That particular night, my teenagers had come down from their rooms to the kitchen (located near my office) for a snack break. I noticed my thirteen-year-old daughter staring at me from the kitchen and felt her walking toward my office as my eyes remained fixed on my computer screen. She touched me on the arm and pleaded, "Mom, I need you to look at me. Please, look up from your computer so you can focus on what I have to say." I stopped what I was doing, almost sad that she had to be the adult in this interaction and unglue me from the monitor. I turned to her and she said, "Let's go over the schedule for tomorrow," and we launched into a short dialogue about the next day's events as I pulled up the iCalendar to jog my memory.

My *child* had to take me off of *my* device. My child. The typical roles were reversed. *She* had to disconnect *me* so that *I* would listen to *her*. No matter the age of your children, I'm certain you can conjure up a number of similar experiences. I continue to work on resisting my strong connection and magnetic draw to my computer, as I'm sure we all do. But really,

I am ashamed to admit this reality. You see, I was not—am not—present with my children when I am glued to a screen. Professor of Psychiatry Daniel J. Siegel and psychotherapist Tina Payne Bryson, authors of *The Power of Showing Up* and *The Whole-Brain Child*, tell us the following:

> Our research and experience suggest that raising happy, healthy, flourishing kids requires parents to do just one key thing . . . Just *show up* . . . Showing up means bringing your whole being—your attention and awareness—into this moment with your child . . . When you do that, you'll be teaching them how to love, and how relationships work. They'll be more likely to choose friends and partners who will see and show up for them, and they'll learn how to do it for others, meaning they'll build skills for healthy relationships, including with their own kids, who can then pass the lesson on down the line through future generations.[1]

At that particular moment, I was not *showing up* for my daughter. Parents, check your own technology use so that you can be proud of the example you set for your kids—so that you can hone your practice of presence. Unplug yourselves when it comes time for those important, and even those seemingly insignificant, face-to-face conversations.

My daughter recently came home from school after her human skills class and shared that she and her classmates had learned how to self-monitor their personal tech usage on various apps. She asked us to self-monitor as a family on a weekly basis. And do you know what? It's shocking to see how our time is divided into usage minutes on various social media and application platforms—and those minutes don't even factor in the time we spend on our laptops. This exercise was a great wake-up call for me, my spouse, and my other teens. Why not check your family usage from time to time?

Let's all agree that it's hard enough to manage your family under the roof of your own home *before* infusing the outside world with its pushes, pulls, media, messages, electronic connectivity and academic and social pressures; suddenly you are parenting in a world that brings the outside world into your home much more frequently—and all at the touch of a button. A generation ago, all parents had to do to limit social access was unplug the landline telephone, but now cell phones, Apple watches, and computer messaging allow for a connection that is continuous and penetrating. Yes, you are still in control of what occurs in your home, but even with the best of intentions, your good parenting can be derailed by strong outside forces and distractions. *By building a solid foundation with your tween or teen that is based on trust, empathy, intention, communication, and understanding, you can start to challenge and overcome some of these outside influences that can become so debilitating.*

The honest truth? This has been the most challenging chapter of this book for us to write. But really, we cannot, in good faith, write a book on parenting behavior without addressing the very real issues wrapped up in the complexities, the dangers, and, yes, even the positive attributes of social media and technology. Admittedly, entire books, scientific studies, statistical analyses, and thousands of articles are written on technology use in our society. And much of the data that has been gathered is so new that we won't fully understand the long-term impacts of technology use until our children are parents themselves. So, in this chapter we have chosen to focus on issues that pertain specifically to your evolving parenting skills—to keeping yourself in check and to prioritizing intention and presence in your approach to technology in your home. (For more up-to-date research and information on prevention in digital media, visit Common Sense Media at commonsensemedia.org).

We will ask you to honestly gauge your own technology use and then urge you to use intentional parenting principles as you navigate the use of technology in your home. When you sense that your kids have been on their devices too much, are you accusatory? Are you angry? Do you threaten? Do you jump to accusations before questioning? We encourage you to dialogue with your family about what tech rules will be upheld in your household and to best determine how your devices won't divide you. Reflect on your parenting practices as they relate to tech, and determine your own dependence on your devices.

Create a Technology Contract

Setting clear expectations around the use of technology sets the foundation for parenting *with intention, not in tension*. One way to do this is to create a family media agreement, which spells out your family's tech rules, and encourage every member to uphold it.

Other technology experts like Chelsea Brown, Certified Cyber Security Expert and Parent Educator, believe that contracts alone are ineffective. Instead she promotes the concept of "Security Practices and Skills for Kids." Brown feels that contract rules are too rigid and do not allow enough flexibility for instruction around the reasons for the rules or their consequences. Contracts are often worded in ways that don't give kids logical consequences that teach correct, alternative behaviors; subsequently, teens don't have what she calls "a redemption plan." In other words, there is no way to learn and then to repair. Tiffany Shlain, author of *24/6: The Power of Unplugging One Day a Week*, adds, "Making a tech contract is a great foundation for putting talking points down; but a tech contract should be collectively revisited every four to six months. You have to look at this as a living document."[2] Brown suggests making a family tech safety plan to come up with the basic foundational rules, and then going through each item on the plan to modify it to reflect consequences. For example, you might implement a three-strike consequence regarding a particular behavior or bad choice you are trying to remedy. Or, if your teen is taking inappropriate photos and texting them, his phone is taken away. Once he feels ready to discuss and subsequently express understanding about what is appropriate to photographically share and what is not, he can earn it back and demonstrate that he has improved his behavior. Most importantly, there needs to be a process in place that allows your teen to earn the device back.[3] Also, just as we positively reinforce following the rules and using good manners when our kids are young, remember to praise the positive use of tech: "That's a nice message of congratulations you sent to your friend," or, "I liked your positive post about being kind," or, "Your post about hard work and teamwork was inspiring."

Try a Disconnection Diet

Did you know that, on average, a teen spends 7.5 hours per day in front of a screen for entertainment purposes and that, over the course of a year, that time cumulatively adds up to 114 days?[4] Fellow parents, let's do the math. That's nearly one third of a year—straight through—plopped in front of a screen!

My friend Amy told me that her daughter, Elise, gave up her cell phone for a month. Elise described what the sacrifice would be like to her mom, cautioning her that it would be harder than staying away from chocolate or caffeine. The challenge meant using an old-fashioned telephone landline for verbal communication with friends after school, having face-to-face conversations when she hung out with her friends (gasp!), and no texting on her computer. She allowed herself email in small doses for homework-related issues. Elise asked Amy if she would join her in the challenge; Amy (albeit reluctantly and painfully) agreed.

Amy characterized the disconnection like a diet; it took discipline and resolve to continue to do it for thirty (very long) days. But she also told me that disconnecting felt kind of illicit—like going on a vacation during her work week. It took more effort and planning to engage with adult friends, and when her kids needed her, they had to go to the school office to use the phone and hope that their mom would be near a landline to take the call. They had to call their dad at work and even resorted to a grandparent once when Amy couldn't be reached. I'll admit that hearing her describe the endeavor made me a little anxious, but, if I'm being honest, also a little bit jealous—kind of like when a parent tells me they want to move their family to a slower-paced environment or take a year to live in another country, and the family actually does it! A lot of us talk about it, but most of us rarely follow through with a plan to actually do it.

Attempt a mini tech vacation for your family. Start small, making a twenty-four-hour initial goal and building up as your family becomes better able to navigate the inherent inconveniences. As a family, discuss the process—the good and the bad—after one day of disconnection. Or, if total disconnection isn't possible, consider simply disconnecting from social media as a family for an agreed-upon period of time. One of us does this annually for a two-month period, and the presence in face-to-face interactions that results from pulling our prying eyes out of other people's lives is worth the discipline it takes to make it happen.

Some families opt to make a certain day of each week tech free. Shlain and her family practice intention in their tech use by taking a "tech Shabbat," a day of rest from devices from sundown Friday to sundown Saturday. This practice is not done for religious reasons, but rather to simply add value to Shlain's family life. For over a decade, Shlain and her family have practiced this ritual, which she describes as the "single best thing I have ever done as a parent and a human, and it is the best day of the week for us all. My [older] teen, who is in her most intense year of high school, cannot wait for [sundown every Friday]." Shlain goes on to explain:

> Humans are not designed to be "on" this much. Even leisure becomes work; we are constantly documenting and captioning. When I'm online I can't get enough. I am in a constant state of never being satisfied. But when I turn things off, I am in a state of appreciation. The time off feels luxurious and long; we all laugh a lot more, we listen to our old-fashioned record player; we are in a better state of being and sleep better Friday night than any day of the week. We ponder the answers to questions that we cannot look up on our phones. Ultimately, my best ideas come on Saturdays. I feel so much more productive because I have given myself a true day off. And the biggest benefit is that I feel the most connected to my family and myself that day.[5]

Shlain tells us that occasionally, one of her kids will complain that she's bored. Her response? "Awesome, that's the runway to creativity."

The Flip Phone Approach

Milad and his siblings had never had social media accounts. All three of them spent their free time working a job and honing their practice of karate. And their phones, well, they looked a little different than those of their peers. Jokingly, Milad called them "ancient," but really a better description would have been practical. Milad's father recognized early that his children needed a way to communicate with their peers and with him, but he also wanted to practice intention in his rules around the use of technology in his home, so each of his kids was given an old-fashioned flip phone. This approach allowed for communication in the form of phone calls and texting, but that's where the limit was drawn; indeed, there was no instant connection to the Internet or mindless browsing of social media. (And yes, you can still purchase flip phones today!) Over the course of his high school years, Milad and I had several conversations about his unique phone. He admitted that, yes, it made him stick out a bit and that he got teased from time to time; that, true, it was occasionally annoying; and that, sure, he missed out on some of the things that didn't happen in person. But more importantly, Milad recognized that over the course of those formative four years, he became accustomed to cherishing in-person dialogue with friends, becoming comfortable conversing with adults, and being okay with missing the sometimes dramatic events that played out on Snapchat and Instagram. He saw that it contributed to the laser-sharp focus he had on attaining his goal of becoming a blackbelt and knew that, while a sacrifice, it positively impacted his work—in and out of the classroom. Parents, consider challenging yourselves to follow this family's lead. What would life be like if your teen used a flip phone?

Navigate Tech Like a Tech Exec

While assumptions might lead us to believe that the homes of technology executives are aglow with blue light, permitting liberal use of devices, the reality is interestingly quite the opposite in many cases.

"Every evening Steve [Jobs] made a point of having dinner at the big long table in their kitchen, discussing books and history and a variety of things . . . No one ever pulled out an iPad or computer. The kids did not seem addicted at all to devices," recounts Walter Isaacson, author of *Steve Jobs*. The parenting of several other technology CEOs and venture capitalists bears a striking resemblance: "They strictly limit their children's screen time, often banning gadgets on school nights and allocating ascetic time limits on weekends." Tech leader Chris Anderson is quoted saying, "[W]e have seen the dangers of technology firsthand . . . I don't want to see that happen to my kids," and, "This is rule No. 1: There are no screens in the bedroom. Period. Ever."[6] We find it particularly instructive that the very people who think up and produce our ever-evolving technology recognize its pitfalls, and their approach to it in their own homes should give us pause as we navigate its use ourselves.

Post with Intention, Not in Tension

Do you ask permission of your kids when you post photos of them (or even better, when you post a throwback to those adorably embarrassing toddler photos of them wherein you inadvertently agreed to that horrible haircut or dressed them in what is now an embarrassing outfit), or do you paste their accomplishments all over your social media? At some point your kids may not want you to post about them without first running it by them. Would you like it if they posted a snapshot of your morning bedhead and drool-stained chin without asking you? Well, they might feel the same way—even about a post that you find completely innocuous. Do them the courtesy of asking their permission.

Adults and teens should "post with intention."[7] Who do you want to see your post? And, really, what is the point of your post? What do you intend to happen as a result of your post? Is there some knowledge or useful factoid that you are sharing with your audience—your *entire* audience? Shlain comments, "It's not always fun for a kid to see the places where they were not invited or events that they were excluded from."

And she encourages the poster to ask herself, "What need is my post trying to fill?"[8] These considerations are the same for both adults and teens. Put it to your teen this way: if a parent, grandparent, teacher, coach, or classmate would be uncomfortable or, indeed, offended by the post, then don't post and instead reconsider. *Post with intention, not in tension.*

In a recent fascinating article in *The Atlantic*, the authors explore the "Dark Psychology of Technology." After a thought-provoking discussion of social media and politics, the authors suggest a few small but interesting solutions to some of the negative effects that our world is experiencing since the inception and explosion of social media.

> Reduce the contagiousness of low-quality information. Social media has become more toxic as friction has been removed. Adding some friction back in has been shown to improve the quality of content. For example, just after a user submits a comment, AI can identify text that's similar to comments previously flagged as toxic and ask, "Are you sure you want to post this?" This extra step has been shown to help Instagram users rethink hurtful messages.[9]

In fact, one teen with ingenuity, Trisha Prabhu, took the initiative to significantly reduce online bullying by designing an app platform called ReThink. Her goal is to try to stop cyberbullying at its source. After a teen types a post, her program asks, "This message may be hurtful to others. Are you sure you want to post this message?" And due to her research on the impulsivity of the teen brain, her platform reduces the decision to post from 70 percent down to 4 percent, literally thwarting millions of ugly, hurtful, harmful posts from ever being seen.[10]

Encourage your teen to similarly filter himself (or download one of the apps that will do it for him): "Are you sure you want to post this?" Posting text or photos on digital media is like getting a permanent tattoo. The words you or your teen writes—whether on a quick Snapchat or in an Instagram post or in a "private" text message—are anything but quick and private.

Check Your Kids' Social Media and Discuss What You Find

If you pay for the phone, you own the phone. That ownership affords you the right to check texts, posts, and even private messages embedded in apps. Make that message very clear to your teen. So your kids don't feel as though they are being "random drug tested," start by periodically checking their phones at night, once they go to sleep. Phones, as we suggest elsewhere in this book, should be plugged into a common dock each night away from the bedroom (and laptops too, since teens can use all of these devices interchangeably). Purchase an "old-fashioned" bedside alarm clock or clock radio (yes, they still sell those, too!) for your teen if he complains that he needs his phone to wake him up. Here's the key: if you find concerning or questionable content on your teen's phone, don't be quick to punish. Instead, talk with your teen. Express your concerns, fears, and frustrations with how he is expressing himself and suggest alternative and more productive ways for him to communicate appropriately. One middle school principal suggests:

> Parents. It is your number one job as a parent to get in your kids' way at all times. Kids do not deserve privacy without accountability. You own their devices, not them. You should be having the hard conversations with them about life, relationships, their bodies, their futures, etc. It is your responsibility to provide social and emotional support, help build coping skills, and monitor their activities, especially online. Please stop actively working against the schools and start working with us. We are not the enemy [when we alert you to what we find on your child's phone]. We are trying to fulfill the role of both parent and educator in many situations, and that is a very delicate and difficult line to walk . . . Inform yourself on how to use certain apps. Keep up with what apps are the most downloaded in the App Store. Make your kids show you their content and

conversations and explain to you what is going on. Then give them advice.[11]

Model Good Tech Behavior— Especially at the Dinner Table

It's time for some honesty. Parents, do you bring tech to the kitchen table (sure, you just need to check the time), doctor's waiting rooms (there's just *one* email that you need to read), car, grocery store, or restaurants (we know, that call was *really* important) rather than interacting with your kids? Interestingly enough, research has shown that parents bring their technology to family meals as much as two times more often than their kids do.[12] "Do as I say, not as I do" might have worked its flawless magic when your kids were younger, but if we're really being honest, what your kids see you do with technology will appear acceptable to them. *And what teenager doesn't have a fine-tuned radar in spotting hypocrisy?*

Be intentional about agreeing upon using (or eschewing) technology at the dinner table so that each member of your family can buy in. A 2017 study found that "the mere presence of one's smartphone may reduce available cognitive capacity and impair cognitive functioning, even when consumers are successful at remaining focused on the task at hand." Unfortunately, while in some ways devices connect us, in those moments where presence is a valuable commodity, we are inherently disconnected and unavailable.[13] Shlain adds unequivocally, "There should be no technology at the dinner table. A family meal is about a thirty-minute experience out of the whole twenty-four-hour day. Referencing a phone and looking something up also leads to distraction. If one person at the communal meal pulls out of the tech-free deal, it is permission to tune out, for everyone to use their phone, and then we are all out of the experience."[14] In our own families, we support abstention from the use of tech at the dinner table, although admittedly it isn't always easy to enforce.

On the other hand, some families find that the presence of devices, when their role is unambiguous, is acceptable. According to The Family Dinner Project's *Eat, Laugh, Talk: The Family Dinner Playbook*, it's okay to have tech at the table in a limited capacity. Technology is "part of the tapestry of modern life. We recognize that technology at the table can sometimes serve as a bridge to conversation by breaking down barriers and opening communication. Instead of a blanket ban, [consider] options to modify and minimize its use so that it doesn't hijack this important time."[15]

"A starting point at the dinner table is for parents and kids to agree on the rules. For some families, there may be a strict no-tech policy, with the idea that dinner should be a time when you focus on each other. You might agree to use technology in a limited fashion—such as consulting phones to resolve factual disagreements that come up at dinner—while others may share interesting photos or emails at the table as a way to talk about their days."[16]

It's Hard to Leave the School Day Behind

In Chapter 2, we challenged you to recall the details of your childhood. And now, in a much more abbreviated exercise, we ask you to add technology use at that time into the mix. After the school bell rang when you were a tween or teen, you probably hopped on your bike or walked or maybe squeezed into the smelly back seat of a carpool—likely heading directly home or perhaps to the park. Your after-school "screen time" might have involved watching a TV show or an after-school special for a bit before you did a little homework, then you took a break when you were called in for dinner, and then maybe you finished your homework. More "technology" use could have meant talking on the landline phone with friends, listening to the radio or a CD, or watching a TV show. Communication during school (and in class) meant whispering when the teacher's back was turned; passing handwritten notes; or chatting at lunch, recess, in the hallways between classes, or in the bathroom. *But, now, the digital age has made it impossible to leave school and friends behind, even when our kids are home from school.*

One high school social science teacher observes the overwhelming impact of technology on teens:

> I feel the countless effects of technology on all of us, but especially on the lives of children and teens. I admit that these impacts are both positive and negative, and some more obvious than others, but in many cases I am not sure that adults and professionals have all the answers yet to the problems that are caused by our rapidly changing technological and digital world . . . [Our generation] came from a world that was not so dominated by digital culture and social media, leading to, at worst, ignorance to the role and impact of technology and, at best, an understanding that is limited by generational experience. Technology creates . . . an incredibly powerful tool of comparison that is seemingly unhealthy for human life. This tends to be exacerbated in high school students who are at the peak point of comparison in their lives . . . Social media has put that phenomenon of comparison on steroids, and for students who are trying to figure themselves out in real time while at the same time attempting to fit in and be accepted by their peers, it creates tremendous pressures. The students who seem to have the most success academically and socially really do seem to balance their technological use, beyond simply limiting the distraction of a cell phone during class hours.[17]

Social media has created an instant, live-and-in-real-time connection for our teens. The moment a classmate posts, those who follow her can see exactly what is on her mind. Sleepovers, birthday parties, or activities that exclude kids are now posted for public consumption. Bullying and superficial analysis of pictures abound, and they can be so mortifying that kids are terrified to bring the embarrassing moments to their parents. But there are ways to practice good parent etiquette in order to help your kids be sensitive and kind in social media interactions.

About Maya

Social media had hurt Maya. A floater in high school without one distinct group of friends, Maya moved around among the cliques, which she described as full of drama. Rather than becoming consumed with group dynamics that brought her down, she chose instead to eat lunch with different girls each day and to invite them over one at a time to hang out. But that approach wasn't always easy. Photos of parties that she wasn't invited to, group texts that singled out individuals in a persecutory way, hurtful messages directed at her—these social media encounters were damaging. But Maya also understood, after talking with her mom, that there is a fine line between posting (happy) activities going on in your day and posting images or words that hurt. Maya was so sensitive to that uncomfortable feeling of being excluded that she decided to be extra sensitive when she and her mom were planning a big celebration—her sweet sixteen.

Budget and space restrictions limited the number of classmates Maya could invite from school. She had a large class and had to exclude about one third of her classmates, both girls and boys. In order to limit potential hurt feelings, Maya and her mom took many preventative measures, most notably making the event device free: texting, photos, and social media would not be allowed at the party. Of course, students at school would eventually hear about the event, and the week before many did. If asked about the guests invited, Maya patiently explained the truth: that she wished she could have invited the whole class, but her parents limited her numbers and that she was so sorry.

Maya's story now takes a socially sad turn. A few days before her event, a disgruntled classmate with hurt feelings posted a damaging image on Instagram with the caption: "For anyone who invited the entire grade to a sweet sixteen except for like fourteen people, please go away. No one wants you here." Devastated, Maya burst into tears, broke out in a full body rash, and didn't want to go to school the next day. While this classmate was obviously hurt from being left out, she chose to express her anger through social media in an accusatory manner—an inappropriate way to publicly express her feelings. This experience was used as a teachable moment for the teens.

The Digital Footprint and College Admission

We think it's safe to say that, in theory, we all understand that our social media posts are collectively creating our unique digital footprint. What we put "out there" reflects who we are. Often, even after taking down a hastily composed or against-our-better-judgment post, the damage has already been done, as even the most "private" posted images or words can still be screenshotted in a matter of seconds and then distributed. But the teenage mind doesn't always grasp the gravity of this reality.

In 2017, Harvard University famously rescinded multiple accep- tances based on ill-advised social media posts. Ten recently accepted students learned that they would no longer be a welcome addition to campus after they posted racially charged and sexually inappropriate comments to a private Facebook group chat.[18]

Parents, take heed. Your teen can encounter the ramifications of imprudent posting even years down the line. In a poignant commentary about etiquette on social media, Jeff Schiffman, Director of Admission at Tulane University, writes: "The thing that we have the most zero tol- erance for is when you act like a real jerk to someone on social media. Any form of cyberbullying, making fun of classmates and teachers on your [social media], or any kind of cruelty in the virtual world is a surefire way to have your admission rescinded. How you behave when you think no one else is watching tells a lot about your character, and if we get word that you've been cruel to someone else, expect to make alternative future plans."[19]

Tech's Not *All* Bad

My family loves the board game Ticket to Ride: both the youngest and the oldest among us enjoy it equally, and it never ceases to bring out the competitive nature that is seemingly ingrained in our shared DNA. But recently, my kids and husband discovered that there was a phone app version of the game. You can be certain that I panicked, resisted, and fought the idea, sure that this technology had robbed us of our fun, shared, gather-around-the-table family experience—but I could not have been more wrong. One Sunday morning a few weeks ago (and a few years after we started playing Ticket to Ride), my husband and two younger kids, both teenagers, were cuddled up on the living room couch, each with a device in hand while they played together, talked, and cracked up with laughter and friendly heckling. I realized then that our Ticket to Ride board game was not replaced, just streamlined. In fact, according to my daughter, the app enhanced the experience: it kept score and even allowed her to make her moves after school and my husband to play some of his moves virtually with her on nights when he worked late at the office. This fun shared game application has just morphed into another way for us to connect and *not* disconnect, as I had originally feared.

And you'd have thought I would have learned that lesson from the Xbox dilemma that preceded it. We were the last family on the block to own the game console, despite the fact that our kids begged us for far too many birthdays and holidays. We feared that they would become video game addicts, giving up playing outside and being active in the fresh air over the lure of electronic games. Initially, we set up a reward system whereby in order to play thirty minutes on the Xbox they had to log an equal thirty minutes of outside time. It quickly became clear to us, however, that the Xbox was just another form of competitive and surprisingly interactive play. They mostly gravitated toward Guitar Hero and rock and roll games (despite their real-life lack of talent in the music arena!) and also Xbox sports games during which they laughed, joked, and competed with friends (regardless of whether the friends were actually athletic or not!). Madden Football and FIFA Soccer were the main games that consumed them in an interactive, laughter-inducing kind of way. We had less to fear than we had anticipated. In fact, our high school son still plays live Xbox games with many of his friends on the weekends when they cannot get together face-to-face. He shouts and calls out players and moves, laughs and interacts a lot, and has a great time. My husband and I are pleasantly surprised at how interactive the Xbox sports games actually are (even though we and he really do prefer participating in live sports games).

A recent *Forbes* article outlined some ways that parents can use tech to unite a family and not overtake the home. A home that is full of enticing off-screen options such as engaging board games; collective cooking opportunities; group art projects (in our home we have an oversized family coloring book that we leave out with markers and a perpetually unfinished puzzle that is always inviting involvement); and social outdoor activities such as a basketball hoop, a croquet set, Corn Hole, or Spikeball can help peel eyes off of devices and invite outdoor recreational play.[20] If your space or budget permits, a pool table (tabletop or life-size), Ping-Pong table, or foosball set up in the garage or family room also serve as ideal tech-free distractors.

Talk about tech so it is not a taboo topic that no one wants to broach. "Invite informal discussions of what your kids are up to online. Who's their favorite YouTuber? What show are they streaming now? What is their favorite app at the moment?" said Theresa Desuyo, a digital family expert interviewed for the *Forbes* article. Dr. Scott Noorda, also interviewed for the article, suggests discussing tech as a tool with your teens: "Go online with your kids to find recipes together . . . Teach them to use goal-tracking apps to help establish good habits."[21]

Technology is not all bad, and we know it. It can unite us and help build community. Tech offers us access to the world and connectivity at our fingertips. Since tech continues to become increasingly entangled in the fabric of our lives and our teens' lives, let's also remember the good things. We know how great a positive message or photo feels, how a shared article motivates us, how a couple can meet through an app and get married, how a video of a military family reuniting can make us cry, how a human moment of paying it forward inspires us, how happy news in turn makes us happy—and how we feel more connected to the good in our world when we read it. This chapter has offered many warnings and cautionary tales about how tech can harm this generation of kids, but there is also so much good that comes from it.

Parent as if the Filters Are Gone Tomorrow

Brown suggests that when it comes to navigating the tricky digital world with our kids, we parent them as if we will relinquish all control tomorrow—as if they were to become an adult tomorrow. "Don't parent from a place of fear. Parent your kids as if tomorrow, all filters don't work so they are prepared to make good choices [now] . . . Proactively help them develop skills to get better, to self-regulate, and to learn and grow from digital mistakes that they *will* make."[22] After all, in practicing good parenting, aren't we teaching our teens the skills they'll need to make good choices in all aspects of their lives and preparing them to be future adults? They will falter, and we will use ideas from this book to navigate teachable moments. Technology is here to stay, and while it can be a scary vortex for parents who are trying to keep up with the latest TikTok craze or whatever else just ended, it is better to be in the know and to face it with intention than to ignore or complain about the damage it is causing.

CHAPTER 7:

TEACH YOUR TEEN TO USE GOALS

At 7:47 AM every morning, we hit the second stoplight on the fourth exit of Interstate 5. And it is at that very moment that my daughter pipes up, almost conditioned to do so: "My goal for the day is to help my teacher." My younger daughter dutifully follows: "My goal is not to whine." They inevitably glance at each other, satisfied and ready to tackle the day.

Goal setting has become not only a daily practice in our home but also an annual practice in both my business and my marriage, largely as a result of what I have learned during my experience counseling high school students. And while the goals of a preschool or an elementary school student might be markedly different from those of a middle school or a high school student, and those even still from an adult, the exercise—for everyone—is confidence building and, most importantly, empowering. Fellow parents, as you practice intentional parenting—parenting led by a compass—goal setting should nestle its way into your parenting tool arsenal. Encourage your tween or teen to think through—even visualize—what it is that she wants to accomplish, and just as importantly, how she's going to get there.

Do you ever keep a to-do list with pen and paper or on an electronic device? If you do, you can relate to the surge in motivation that accompanies recording even the most mundane of tasks. Take the car in for an oil change? Well, I wrote it down, so . . . And if you know what I'm talking about, then you can also identify with that ever-so-satisfying feeling when it comes time to cross something off of that list. I'm pretty sure the corners of my lips curl upward ever so slightly whenever I draw my pen straight through an item or hit delete on my digital list. It's almost as if I've waged a miniscule battle with each task, and with every strikethrough, I've recorded a glorious victory. The same goes for goal setting. There is something intrinsically empowering about writing out a goal. When we put out into the world that we want to achieve something, well, then our determination hardens, and we have no choice but to take that first step.

Setting Goals Contributes to Intention and Provides a Roadmap

Beginning each day with intention—with an idea of what you want to accomplish—sets the tone for empowerment and achievement. In a world full of negative feedback, damaging media messages, and discouraging interactions, goal setting instead welcomes the day on a positive and hopeful note. It not only teaches all of us to reach for our dreams but also gives some structure and a roadmap to get there.

People who think about and record their goals, and then set measurable objectives to achieve those goals, are much more likely to achieve what they set out to accomplish. So you can be sure that every fall, my students are becoming inspired as they diligently record their goals for the coming school year. Some begin enthusiastically, furiously recording what has so long been in their heads but has never been put to paper, memorializing their intention, making a contract with themselves, and therefore urging them on. *I want to achieve an A in AP Chemistry. I would love to make varsity volleyball. I'd like to become color guard captain. I intend to write for the school newspaper.* Others come to the process begrudgingly. *I've never thought about what I want to achieve. I know what I want to achieve, but I have never considered how I might get there.*

I chuckle to myself every fall during the goal-setting process. It's because I love goal setting with the hesitant students the most. I have students set three goals, each with three measurable objectives. The first goal inevitably is an adjustment for them; it takes some time to solidify and then it takes even more time to come up with three concrete steps that will get them to the finish line. Around goal number two, though, the light bulb visibly brightens, and students can't help but mask a little smile as they settle in to the process and feel the intrinsic motivation.

This happens every time without fail. As they think through the potential for achievement, they start to feel empowered and get excited. They have direction. (If your teen does not work with an educational consultant or therapist, or if your child has never done a goal-setting exercise before, we encourage you to try setting goals with measurable objectives as you embrace the plan set out here.)

Establishing a Foundation and Understanding

Another reason that goal setting is an essential counseling and parenting tool is that the process allows adults to understand what children want for themselves. As a counselor, I develop a clear picture of what it is that *they* want to achieve, and I establish a foundation from which to work. If I am unclear on their goals, then *my* assumptions are, albeit unintentionally, guiding my work rather than their true intentions and desires for themselves. For instance, I might assume that a student ultimately wants to attend one of the most selective institutions in the country and therefore gear my advice and our work toward that assumed goal. But instead, much to the contrary, that particular student's goal is to attend a school at which he will receive considerable merit aid and at which he has the ability to rise to the top of his class. How different those two goals are—and how a student's goals can be disrupted with an inappropriate assumption!

Parents, think about your own lives. Have you ever sat down and written out where you want to be in the next year? Five years? Most of us haven't. Why not try? There exists incredible power in modeling this type of intentionality to your children.

A few years ago, I instituted this practice with my husband. Drawing from what I've learned about the power of goal setting, we decided to adopt a new tradition to set family goals every New Year's Day. We review what we would like to improve in our family—it might be more family dinners, adding a weekly Friday night movie night, or relating to fitness or finances—and we set goals coupled with measurable objectives at which to chip away throughout the coming year. I do it for my business, too. Where do I want to be in twelve months—but more importantly how am I going to get there? What are the steps that I will take to make that happen? Parents, try adopting this goal-setting idea in your own homes whenever there is a crossroads or an upcoming milestone that demands it.

About Gwen

A few years ago, I set goals with Gwen. Passionate about bringing creative writing to elementary school-aged children, Gwen was leading creative writing and poetry workshops around her city, but she wanted to reach a broader audience and formalize what she was doing. But she didn't know where to begin. We began with her overarching, "big picture" goal—what she wanted to achieve. *Grow my creative writing workshops to reach more children.* Then we had to move on to identifying three measurable steps to get there.

What Is a Measurable Objective?

The necessity that objectives are measurable can't be stressed enough. For instance, a student might want to achieve an A in United States History. When queried how he intends to get there, that student will likely say, "Study harder." But what does that mean? How does he know that he is studying harder? How can he be sure that what he does going forward is measurably any different from what he is doing now? (And clearly what he is doing now isn't working or he would not have set this goal in the first place.) Studying harder is not a measurable objective, and therefore, it isn't a useful one. A better objective might be to study for one extra hour every Sunday afternoon. Or maybe a student has been doing his math homework last every night, when he's tired and burned out from his other homework. Perhaps doing his math homework first every night, when he is most fresh and alert, would contribute to a raise in his homework grade, correlating to a raise in his overall math grade.

So back to the example about the writing workshops. Gwen decided upon her first objective: *reach out to more libraries*. While a good start, this was still not a measurable objective. She tried again: *reach out to five new libraries by December 31*. This objective was measurable, so it worked. Gwen moved on to her next objective. For her second objective, she started to think about conducting her workshops in new locations beyond libraries—in order to reach different audiences. Knowing that some low-income communities were located near her home, she chose to reach out to three nonprofit organizations to see if they would allow her to use her workshop format to teach children living in those communities. She gave herself the deadline of March 31.

For her last objective, she wanted to come up with a way to first draw kids into the idea of creative writing and then let them know about her workshops—inviting them after they'd seen what they could eventually accomplish. She decided to set up "slam poetry" nights with the plan to advertise her workshops at these events. Her final objective was to set up four slam poetry nights by the end of the school year.

Over time, Gwen's workshops grew as a result of her goal setting and her commitment to seeing those goals through. Not only did she reach more kids, inspiring scores of young people, but she later parlayed her momentum into creating a nonprofit organization that introduces young people to creative writing.

Setting Goals with Your Teen

Setting goals with your teen can be an incredible, bonding experience. *When a parent sits down with a child solely for the purpose of learning what the child wants to achieve, the teen feels heard and knows that she has a voice.* Much like the process of setting goals in our own college counseling offices, when you and your teen set goals together it allows you to both start from the same place—helping you to know exactly how to encourage your teen in a way that makes her feel valued.

Goals can be short term or long term, and when I goal set with students, I don't limit the time frame. Start by helping your teen understand the difference between a goal and an objective. Remember, a goal is the "big picture" thing that your teen will aim to achieve. An objective is a measurable step to get to that goal. You can give your teen examples of non-measurable objectives, like studying harder, and measurable objectives, like visiting a teacher's tutorial or office hours before each test.

I like to set one goal with students and then identify its accompanying three objectives before moving on to the second goal; your teen can also start by focusing solely on one goal and its objectives rather than three goals at once. Especially if your teen has never recorded his goals before, he will likely struggle making his first goal. Carefully listen and be still in the silence. He will eventually come up with something, and too many suggestions from an adult will take ownership of the process from him.

When he moves from the goal into the objectives, challenge him to set objectives that he is not currently doing. Often, I'll see students who breeze through identifying the objectives because they list the things that they are already doing. But what's the good in that if it hasn't yet gotten them to their goal? For instance, maybe your child's goal is to increase her speed in soccer, as she hopes to be a recruited athlete. For her first objective, she writes down that outside of practice, she will run a timed two miles, two times per week—but the trouble is that she is already doing this. Encourage her to either identify a different objective or to challenge herself more with the objective that she is already doing. In this case, perhaps the teen can run a timed two miles three days per week outside of practice.

Troubleshooting Objectives

Sometimes, a student will get stuck during the objective setting. He has considered what more he can do to work toward a goal, but even still he is unable to identify appropriate objectives. When this happens, I like to approach the process from a different vantage point—namely, what is currently keeping the student from reaching his goal? When I query him this way, he is able to approach the goal from the back end; rather than adding things that he is not yet doing, he identifies how he can significantly alter his current approach.

About Arvan

Arvan's goal was to earn a B+ in Honors Algebra II, a class in which he was struggling and one in which he found little interest. After deciding to visit his teacher's tutorial hours to go over each test and to do seven extra practice problems every Sunday (adding in things he was not yet doing), he was stuck on his third objective. I approached it from the back end—changing his current approach. What was standing in the way of him getting that B+? Arvan admitted that because he disliked math, he was not disciplined when it came time to do his homework. Every time he heard the "ding" of a text message on his phone, he happily gave in to the distraction. But this resulted in little continuous focus and in getting off track. Arvan's third objective, then, was to leave his phone in a different room while working on his Honors Algebra II homework, giving himself a designated ten-minute phone break after forty-five minutes of homework. Arvan worked diligently to implement this goal over the course of an entire semester, and when he returned at the end of the school year, he not only raised his grade to a B+ but also encountered the unexpected side effect of becoming less dependent upon his phone. Having enjoyed the peace that leaving it in an adjacent room had provided, Arvan went one step further and made the choice to implement more scheduled phone breaks throughout the week—beyond simply when he was doing his homework.

When the goal setting is complete, encourage your child to put her written goals in a place that she will encounter often. We recommend thumb tacking them to a bulletin board, taping them to the bathroom wall, or hanging them anywhere that your teen often passes, so that she can continue to be inspired and reminded. The constant interface with her goals will keep her accountable to herself—and not to you. Sometimes being a good parent means backing off. Try to.

Creating a Tangible Vision

When we constantly observe a visual representation of our future, we can't help but be motivated to work toward whatever that vision might be. If I want to reach a certain mileage in my running, and every morning when I roll out of bed that number is staring right back at me, taunting my snooze button, I'm more likely to throw on my running shoes. Try this with your child: allow him to pin up inspirational quotes and pictures that depict his goals, creating a tangible vision for his future. Many of our students enjoy posting quotes and images all over their bedroom and bathroom walls, mirrors, ceilings, bulletin boards, and even computer screensavers. Whether your teen's saying is a Winston Churchill quote ("I have nothing to offer but blood, toil, tears, and sweat") or a quote from the *Hamilton* musical ("I am not throwing away my shot") or simply "Carpe Diem," inspirational messages can pump anyone up. Some parents even allow their teens to paint a chalkboard wall in their bedrooms that can display their own musings in chalk or to hang a white board that can be updated with meaningful quotes. These can be sage words from musicians, athletes, authors, and famous—or not-so-famous—people. Seeing these quotes—whether printed out in large computer fonts or scribbled across a piece of binder paper—cannot help but inspire students and serve as constant reminders of what they are aiming for in life. Meaningful quotes uplift and enhance a bad day, a disappointing grade, or an argument with a friend. Each day your child can wake up and start over again, knowing these words of support are there to enhance positivity and perseverance. These tangible mottos serve as constant reminders of what they intend to achieve. (Parents, you can even try this on your own, too!)

Assessing and Revising Goals

Even the most focused among us can attest to the fact that some goals are reached on time, some are achieved late, and some are never attained at all. And in that lies the beauty of the process. We learn from our hard work—and just as importantly, we might even learn from our lack of hard work. Assessing and revising goals must be a part of the goal-setting process. It is in this space that we learn and adjust.

While we discussed failure in Chapter 3, it is worth briefly mentioning failure here. *It is important to view an unreached goal not as a failure but instead as a call to make an adjustment.* Perhaps the objective was not realistic. Or maybe in the midst of working toward the goal, a bigger, more important one arose.

The assessment and revision process is an important one because it calls for honesty and an assessment of priorities. It also allows your teen to identify what is working and what isn't—and to return to the drawing board to come up with another plan that might work even better. Frequent assessment and revision of goals is a necessary part of the process and shouldn't be avoided simply because your teen fears admitting that she didn't achieve exactly what she set out to achieve. We recommend at the very least to revisit goals every six months, but this time frame may vary depending upon how short or long term the goals are.

Goal Setting Process Review

1. Set your goal(s), which are the big picture achievements you are working toward.

2. Create measurable objectives, which are the steps you will take to work toward the goal(s).

3. Troubleshoot objectives if necessary. If you get stuck, approach identifying objectives from the back end, asking what is standing in the way of the goal.

4. Create a tangible vision.

5. Assess to see if you are on track to meeting your goal, if adjustments need to be made, or if the goal is achieved.

Consider goal setting as initiating a snowball effect. Like a snowball that begins small, growing exponentially as it picks up speed racing down a mountain, goal setting is inherently a habit that begets bigger and bigger achievements each time it is practiced. Readers, help foster this mindset in your future-adult teen. Goal setting is a practiced art. It takes discipline and focus to endure the process of setting goals, but in turn, it likewise fosters discipline and focus. Helping your teen practice goal setting, and eventually adopting it as a treasured habit, will set him up for a lifetime of intentional action and positivity.

CHAPTER 8:

INSTILL THE IDEA THAT SCHOOL IS A JOB

Good afternoon, Mr. and Mrs. G.,

As the AP U.S. History teacher at Dover High School, I have the pleasure of having your son in my class. I wanted to send you a quick note of thanks for the wonderful job you have done in raising your son. Every class period, Max demonstrates a superior level of understanding regarding the material through his willingness to engage in class discussions, providing nuanced responses that reveal his superior critical thinking skills. While Max maintains an excellent sense of humor and an ability to not take himself too seriously, I do recognize what hard work he applies both within and outside the classroom setting. So again, I just wanted to send a quick note of thanks for the excellent job Max has demonstrated this year.

All the best,

John H.

We begin Chapter 8 with this heartwarming note that was indeed received by one of our clients for a reason—because it exemplifies, perhaps even better than we can, the impact that following your parent compass can have on students and their teachers alike. How would you feel to receive an unexpected email like this about your child, commending you on your parenting? Fellow parents, your personal academic goals for your child should not be set in terms of her particular grades or GPA. Your child's success should be determined by whether or not she works to her personal potential; it should be measured by the effort she puts in—whether or not she likes the subject or the teacher (hey, Max planned to major in physics but this letter came from a history teacher)—and in the curiosity she displays. Your teen should find her own personal best and work up to that. And your job? *Model grit, humor in the face of challenge, and resilience; encourage effort over outcome.* Remember, a "B" for one student may be a great achievement, while a "B" for another might be evidence that she is not trying hard enough. Know your teen and support and encourage her to work at her personal best.

Recently, a teacher candidly shared with us the sad reality that she sees occur when parents fail to practice good parenting habits, putting immense pressure on their kids to achieve rather than meeting their kids where they're at: "Some kids feel like they have to be 'perfect' and will somehow fail their parents if they don't get straight A's and eventually get into a prestigious university. At this point, nothing surprises me anymore. Many of my students feel like they have little say in taking on numerous AP/IB classes, even in subjects in which they are not particularly strong. I was [heavily immersed in our school's] International Baccalaureate program . . . and worked with many kids who were in over their heads and didn't want to take on the heavy workload, but [they] were pressured by their parents to be part of the program. I also dealt with many psychological 'melt downs' (including suicide threats) and ethics violations brought on by the pressure. Students tell me they are being forced into career choices that reflect what [their parents] want."[1] Parents, we implore you to hear this cautionary observation. *Being an attuned parent means that instead of having unattainable and unrealistic college dreams for your kids, you encourage your teen to be the best student he can be.*

School Is a Job

As a parent, you wake up every day, probably pour yourself a large cup of coffee (or two if you really need some pep), and show up to your job; maybe it's working at a company, managing the home, volunteering at a nonprofit, or running your own business. Similarly, every student that we meet learns quickly that we believe *school is her job*. And we encourage you to use that same analogy. Just as you work for your children each day (and night, since we can all agree that parenting is actually 24/7), they, too, have a job: to go to school. Be sure you tell them that you don't care about how well (in terms of grades) they do in school as long as they show up, give it their best effort, seek help when needed, do their homework, find some nice friends, build relationships with a few teachers, and stay organized. We don't think that's too much of parents to ask of their teens.

But what makes your student's job particularly challenging—in a different way than yours—is that he has to contend with six, seven, sometimes even eight bosses: teachers and coaches. But there's a concept we share with our students that can make doing the job of school much easier: figure out *how* the teacher wants things, *what* they want, the *way* they want it, and give it back to them *that* way. In our experience, parents who share this wisdom with their children through a personal story from their own school experience (whether positive or negative) can be more impactful in getting the message across.

Teachers are usually transparent in outlining what they expect from students. On the first day of the term, each teacher presents a syllabus delineating the expectations and requirements of the class. These syllabi provide an opportunity for you to have a conversation with your teen about *studying* her teacher-bosses—how each one wants assignments completed and how best to relate to each one. We've gathered some great open-ended questions that you can ask your teen during such conversations. Be sure to gauge her attention span, and if you sense pushback, leave it alone and try to have the conversation again at another time. Your goal is to come across as a helpful, thoughtful teammate:

- How does the teacher seem? Easy, hard, fair, unfair, etc.?

- Have you talked to any upperclassmen who have taken the course before, and what do they say?

- Is the subject one you like/comes easier to you, or is it generally harder for you compared to other subjects?

- Is the teacher enthusiastic and passionate about the material and the course? Or is the teaching style subdued?

- Do students talk a lot in class, or do you just listen and regurgitate the material?

- Does the teacher give a lot of homework? Extra credit?

- Does the class have a sit-down exam or final paper/project?

- Does the teacher have office hours or a set time he can meet during tutorials, or can you arrange a meeting with him before school or during lunch or break?

- Does the teacher prefer email? What is her general communication style with students?

- Where do you sit in this class? Assigned or unassigned?

School Is Also a Place to Practice Life Skills

If teens can't learn life skills at middle and high school, under the safety net of living under our roofs to help support them when they fail or falter, then where else will they learn life skills and how to make good choices? Throughout middle and high school teens learn interpersonal communication, problem-solving, teamwork, relationship building with peers and teachers, critical thinking, self-advocacy, hard work, written and oral communication skills, time management, independence, responsibility, curiosity, and sacrifice, among other things. And school is also a place where teens will make mistakes and experience disappointments: hurt a friend's feelings; break someone's heart or have theirs broken; be academically dishonest or be disappointed in finding out that someone else has been; and experience academic failures or social, athletic, and extracurricular disappointments. Of course, there will be successes, too. Enduring these experiences in a "safe" environment, before they head off to the real world, allows them to process the events and make adjustments to their responses over time.

About Casey

Senioritis had taken hold of Casey. Lazy and checked out, he had gained a reputation of cutting corners and partying a bit too much. He was well liked by his peers, social, and popular, but he was not very motivated. And senior year he made an unfortunate choice; a teacher caught him blatantly cheating on a test. He was called to sit in front of the school ethics board, which was made up of peers he knew and did not know, and his punishment was decided: he would not be allowed to finish the school year on campus and would not walk at graduation. Instead, he had to complete his work remotely from home. This infraction would remain on his permanent high school record. He was terribly embarrassed and ashamed, and his parents were obviously disappointed, too. How our teens react to failure, take ownership, and move forward from the mistakes that they make help define them. This unpleasant period in Casey's life made him look closely at his bad choice, accept his punishment, and demonstrate remorse. He wrote a letter to his classmates, apologizing for his dishonesty, and had to live with the public humiliation suffered from this bad decision. That "little voice" reminder was now permanently in his head—his conscience—as a future reminder not to make the same mistake again.

School Is a Lot Like Weight Lifting and Recovery

Lisa Damour, psychologist and parenting author of *Under Pressure: Confronting the Epidemic of Stress and Anxiety in Girls*, helpfully analogizes each year of school to a weight-lifting exercise in the gym: at the beginning of first grade, students are handed a set of weights that feel heavy. These small kids think, "Ooh, that is hard to lift," and struggle to exercise their muscles. But little by little and as the school year progresses, and certainly by the last day of first grade, the weights come to feel much lighter than they did on day one; in fact, sometimes there is no real effort exerted at all when lifting those end-of-the-school-year weights—the lifting has been mastered. Then the summer arrives and a deeper recovery period happens. At the start of second grade, the students are handed a new, slightly heavier set of weights and the routine repeats itself, and so on and so on until kids have graduated from every year of their schooling. Just as a gym goer works his way up to heavier and heavier weights and more strenuous exercises after a lot of practice, so, too, does the student.[2]

But just as the weights are important to master (school), so is the recovery process (downtime). Week after week simply working out at the gym becomes monotonous and tedious, and it can cause great fatigue, pain, and burnout. So, it is equally important to make time to recover from the strenuousness of exercise. To do that, we hydrate, rest, take breaks, and breathe. Students at every age also need sufficient downtime in order to recharge, rest, turn off their brains, and relax.[3] Parents, use this analogy when empathizing with your teens regarding school. And practice good parent etiquette by monitoring your teen, making sure she has enough downtime to do what helps her de-stress, decompress, and relax once she is home from school and in the summer.[4] (More on other recovery ideas in Chapter 5 under the section "Playtime, Downtime, and Family Time.")

Helping Your Teen Build Teacher Relationships

Sometimes students forget that their teachers have lives outside of the four walls of the classroom. Teachers go to the movies on the weekend, coach athletic teams, have families of their own, and make Target runs—just like you do. I've observed more times than I can count students bumping into a teacher at the grocery store, the dry cleaner, and even the school parking lot only to freeze up, unsure of what to do or say when they encounter a teacher out of context.

Teens can fortify good teacher relationships in many ways. Let's start with the simplest: by saying the words, "Thank you," at the end of each class. We'll say that again so that it really sinks in: *saying the words, "Thank you," at the end of each class goes a very long way.* You'd be surprised at how few students make the extra effort to convey these two words. Yet teachers remember the kids who are polite and appreciative. Think about it this way: Who *doesn't* like to be on the receiving end of a little gratitude, and honestly, who doesn't feel better after offering it? I am a nut for my exercise spin class (you know those stationary bikes that go nowhere but you still feel exhausted when you're done?), and I've employed this strategy at the conclusion of every class that I take; I actually feel better when I've gone out of my way to let a hard-working instructor know that I appreciate them—and not surprisingly, instructors start to recognize me and remember my name. Likewise, encourage your teen to express gratitude. (You've instilled basic etiquette in him from a very young age, so why shouldn't he translate that to his "school job"?) And when he sees any teacher or coach in the hallway, at lunch, in the parking lot, or, yes, at Target, a simple, "Hello, Ms. Smith," is entirely appropriate. But maybe more importantly, a teen who is comfortable conversing with superiors—with her teacher-bosses—is a teen who, eventually, will be comfortable speaking up and advocating for herself with college professors and, one day, with her bosses at work.

You can also try to role-play if your teen is concerned about how to better connect with his teachers. In counseling sessions, we often role-play and find that it can be a useful tool for our students to practice what they want to say to a teacher and to anticipate how a teacher may respond. *Thinking about a conversation and actually practicing one are different experiences entirely.* Suggest or offer to role-play, and if your teen is receptive, take the time to actually do it.

Facilitating Your Teen's Classroom Self-Advocacy

How would you feel about a colleague who habitually jumped in to inform your boss about *your* projects, *your* concerns, and *your* problems before you could get a word in edgewise? Would you feel empowered? Or would you feel helpless? Would you have positive feelings about your colleague? Or would you resent him? Exactly. Parents, instead of voicing your teen's concerns, fixing her problems, or coming to her rescue when she fails or falters, equip her with the tools to deal with these situations on her own. When there is an academic problem in high school, your teen should be the first one to go to her teacher. One of the worst things you can do for your child is to circumvent her by calling her teacher or emailing on her behalf. Sure, sit beside her as she crafts an email (if she asks you to) or role-play at home to prepare for a face-to-face meeting with the teacher, but *do not step in for her in high school.* Instead, teach her to do it herself. Her teachers expect it, and your job is to prepare her for adulthood by entrusting the communication to her. (The only exception to this would be, of course, if there were some impropriety or safety issue that required parental involvement.)

A dean at a major research university candidly described his observation: "I have noticed a shift in parent behavior toward taking a more direct role when [parents] believe their children are facing a potential challenge. Instead of helping their [college-aged] child navigate the system, they tend to intervene directly and reach out to school officials."[5] Parents, your children are only prepared to self-advocate in college and beyond when they've been given opportunities to practice that skill during the preceding years. So give them that gift.

A high school principal, during our interview with him, described how his school tries to deal with overzealous parents by setting high expectations for their behavior:

> We begin messaging our expectations about students learning to self-advocate during the admission process. I have found that the more times we repeat our expectations and philosophy, the better they "stick" down the road. I talk about it, write about it, send articles, and talk about it some more—all before the ninth graders have matriculated. From there, we continue on with the same messaging from day one. In general, parents get it—at least in principle—and do their best to let their children learn how to effectively approach teachers when they are struggling with something.[6]

Review sessions and office hours allow teens to connect with teacher-bosses face to face. Sometimes tutorials require that a student goes to school early for a zero period or an early start block; sometimes teacher meetings are offered weekly for those students seeking extra help; or schools might offer after-school sessions where students can meet with teachers. Offer to drive your teen to school early or pick him up late if he needs to meet with a teacher (or, if your work schedule prohibits this type of assistance, help your teen figure out alternative transportation). Casually encourage him to take advantage of those times to seek extra help, review missed homework problems, get feedback on written work, or even obtain some clues of what might be appearing on the next quiz or exam. Review sessions always offer little nuggets that can help students in their future testing.

Beyond being a good listener and a sounding board, making suggestions—or planting seeds as we like to call it—can be a good parenting approach to problem-solving. And please note that making suggestions, at the correct time, is not fixing the problem. It involves offering a variety of options when your teen communicates that she is stuck; *it is empowering your teen to do it herself.* Some teens have negative knee-jerk reactions when they feel "bossed around" by a parent; others take parental advice, let it stew and simmer for a while, and then apply it. And many are somewhere in between. Eye rolling and talking back to you are some of the reactions to your seed planting that we know you have experienced. *Knowing your teen and finding the right time to plant these seeds comes as a result of practicing very skilled parent compass following.* Don't worry, we are human, too, and don't always get it right the first time. Please try again if you fail.

Parent Behavior toward Teachers

Gratitude

Parents, just as your teen should be in the practice of expressing genuine gratitude to his "bosses," so should you show appropriate gratitude to your child's teachers. After

Back to School Night or teacher conferences, don't be afraid to send a kind email (or a more personal handwritten note) to each teacher, letting them know you also appreciate their tireless effort. Try to personalize each note with a sentence reflecting on something that the teacher said or on some insight that he provided about your child. You can encourage your child to deliver a small gift card, bring flowers from the garden, or bake something as a nice gesture around the holidays, teacher appreciation week, or certainly when a teacher writes a recommendation for a job or college. An email of gratitude—maybe one per semester—for good work you witness or hear about from your child is always appreciated; consider looping in the administrator or principal if a teacher deserves to be recognized. Teachers always appreciate when their superiors hear or read about a job well done.

If you enjoy it and have the time, volunteering at your child's school as a room parent, in the library, on a parent council, or attending campus parent or grade-level events are other ways to make positive contact with your child's teachers and the school administration. While not imperative, it is always good to be seen around campus as a helpful, friendly contributor or school supporter. Think of it as a more tangible way to express gratitude for the space where your teen spends so much time.

Be a Parent Partner

Notes one public high school teacher:

> Parents tend to believe their children over the perspective of teachers, challenging grades and methods. Yet, when parents take the time to raise issues or voice concerns, if the teacher has a response that explains the motivations behind actions or classroom policies, I have found that [we can reach an understanding] . . . [Y]ou know them better than anyone and have more time with them then we as teachers do, but give the teachers the benefit of the doubt as professionals and the adults in the room. Respect their judgment.[7]

Echoes another during our interview with her: "Don't make the assumption that if your student isn't doing well, it's the teacher's fault."[8]

Become a parent partner. Look at your relationships with your teen's teachers as partnerships working toward common goals: understanding, respect, and growth. Perhaps a teacher has been overly challenging for your child. Maybe there's an issue beyond the scope of what your child can address alone. Or maybe your child has tried to address a concern on his own but without success or a satisfactory solution (such as classroom dynamics or fear of the teacher). It is okay for you to address these issues honestly with your teen's teachers. But, remember that you are a parent *partner*—and partnerships involve compromise, mutual understanding, and the acknowledgment that there are always two sides.

Please, fellow parents, don't attack. Instead, approach the teacher from the perspective that you want to partner together in the interest of your tween or teen. Do not go directly over a teacher's head to a principal or a department head until you have first had a chance to meet with the teacher directly. There is a proper order of events in issues that concern your child in her school, and any good dean or principal will always ask you if you have first gone directly to the teacher. Indeed, a headmaster candidly shared the following with us:

> The more difficult and personal the issue, the more difficult it is for parents to stay out of it. When they see it as something "high stakes," they often cannot help themselves. If they feel the stakes are high or the final outcome is one they do not like, they will often try to reach out to me or another administrator. We will coach them on how to handle it, but we do not get involved unless it is absolutely necessary; for example, if a teacher and student cannot come to a resolution themselves, sometimes a third-party administrator has to help facilitate and mediate. That does not happen very often, though. I always redirect because: 1) I usually do not have any details or knowledge about the situation, and 2)

teachers cannot stand it when parents go straight to the administration, so I try to respect that.[9]

Empathy and Homework

Parents, you are conscientious. We know that because you probably wouldn't be reading this book if you weren't. As such, you know that homework is a necessary—albeit often mundane—part of your student's "school job" and that there is a purpose for it: homework reinforces ideas that are covered in class or introduces cursory topics that are not covered in class. Luckily, schools are increasingly trying to move toward homework being less busywork and more about problem-solving, creative thinking, and multi-step problems that require grit and resilience from students. Some students give up quickly, but teachers want them to push through; homework can also test that. But what do you do if you have a teen who refuses to see homework in this way—as an inevitable part of her very important day-to-day job?

Let me back up and tell you a story that happened just last month. Slightly alarmed by the yelling (peppered with obscenities) I heard coming from outside, I stuck my head out my front door—as any curious neighbor would—to see what was causing the hurling of these choice words. My neighbor's teenage daughter (not a morning person, by the way) had awoken late and on the wrong side of the bed; she was tired and grumpy and hobbling toward her car with one shoe on and one shoe in her hand. Her brother, on the other hand, who had been up equally late doing homework and studying for an important test, was dressed and ready for school with his teeth brushed and bed neatly made and was waiting in the car. He was apparently lamenting his impending tardiness because of his sister. The mother, exasperated, rolled her eyes at me as she tried to usher her daughter into the car. Angry and at an impasse, both parties slammed car doors and made the (rushed) trip to school. My neighbor later explained to me that what I had heard was the end of a heated argument with her daughter surrounding homework, namely the fact that her daughter had chosen not to do her homework—again.

While my neighbor's tactics may not have exemplified the best parenting behavior, she later had an epiphany: her daughter didn't want a frantic tongue lashing and "I told you so" threats; these things weren't going to get her to do her homework, and they certainly weren't going to help her learn. Instead she wanted her mom's empathy. So my neighbor decided to listen to that little voice telling her to calm down, to keep the situation in parental perspective, and to try to turn it into a teachable moment. She realized that she needed to take the long view to parenting; this particular homework assignment wasn't going to break her daughter's academic career. Instead, she needed to help her daughter understand that doing hard and boring things can help in reaching goals. So she switched tactics and tried to reapproach.

When her daughter got home from school that day, my neighbor didn't hesitate before she apologized to her daughter: "Honey, I blew it. I should have first tried to understand your position before jumping to anger. I get it: homework can be boring, and I know that it isn't what you'd choose to do with your evening time. Me neither! But *not* doing your homework isn't helping you. You dig yourself a hole each time you skip it. I remember when I skipped nearly an entire semester of math work, unbeknownst to my parents. I was so behind in my math that it felt hopeless. Back then, there was no way for my parents to check up on my grades, so I just kept pretending that everything was fine when it really wasn't. Not surprisingly, I ended up in summer school that year." Confessing her own faults made her more human to her teen and engendered some solidarity—she'd been there, too. My neighbor, knowing what I do for a living, recalled this series of events to me, reporting that her daughter actually responded positively to her attempt to level with her. The interchange sparked a conversation around ways to make homework more tolerable. More amazingly, she hasn't had a missing homework assignment since. And do you know what? I don't think it was the lesson from her mother's past that moved the daughter to respond; it was instead her mom's flexibility and attempt to apologize and then empathize that urged her to rethink her choices.

Understanding, empathetic, and non-judgmental words are possibly a parent's most magical influential tool, especially when it comes to completing tedious tasks, and homework is no exception. *If and when your kids complain about homework, use empathy to connect and level with them.* You might very well get eye rolls or flat out silence when you approach the homework conversation as an authoritarian, but the conversation will likely go very differently if your teen feels understood. Remind him not to skip it—after all, that will likely end up being the day that the teacher collects it—and, if you can, reference your recollections of homework, so that he feels you can personally relate to his "suffering."

Apart from empathizing, when your kid complains about having too much homework, use the opportunity to investigate home habits. (For more information on homework distraction visit Chapter 5.) Finally, let your kids know that homework is an essential part of school, and that it is what it is: home work.

In our increasingly competitive academic landscape, micromanaging our children as they navigate the classroom can feel like it brings control to an uncertain future—and we understand the pull. We recognize that the parenting strategies we have laid out in this chapter might very well be the hardest ones for some parents to employ—namely, to pull away from what you are so used to doing for your kids—but we also believe that they are doable and, more importantly, that they will contribute to your teen's overall well-being and to your family harmony. You've got this.

CHAPTER 9:
AVOID RANKINGS AND WATCH YOUR MOUTH

A glass bowl filled with neon orange earplugs sits squarely on my desk. Each of my students is invited to reach over to grab a pair for themselves when they visit. The purpose of these noise eliminators is to do just that for each one of them—to silence the noise around them and to encourage them to navigate the college admission process in their own unique way. I encourage my students to carry their earplugs in their backpacks, or tuck them discreetly away in their pencil holders, or nestle them safely into lockers as a tangible reminder to listen to their gut and to do what feels right to them. In part, this means choosing schools for their college list that are a good fit for them based on a variety of measures, including accessibility of professors and mentors, location or proximity to a major city or airport, the major and minor options that align with their goals, presence of student organizations that advance their interests, and how the college prepares its students for the working world upon graduation. (These measures do not include college rankings lists like those produced annually by the *US News & World Report*.)

The Trouble with Relying on Rankings

As counselors, we find that many families are surprised to learn exactly what determines a college or university's ranking on lists like the ones published by the *US News & World Report*. Our hearts sink every time we see families blindly employ these lists to attach misguided value to a name. College rankings are inherently flawed, and relying on them to draw conclusions about the quality of a student's academic experience at a given school is shortsighted. I always gasp in horror (to myself, of course) when I first meet a family and they resolutely present me with an already drafted college list—that is simply a regurgitation of that year's list of the top universities. What is missing, first and foremost, is any consideration of fit for that student, and second, any understanding of what landed those schools in their arbitrary positions on said list. Is Abigail a student who wants hands-on learning in a supportive environment? Perhaps a small liberal arts college is best for her—so why are the top ten public universities the only schools on her college list? Maybe Harrison is looking for a great deal of merit aid. Or Marcus has found specific professors at less recognizable universities that happen to teach in a niche field that interests him. Surely, it would behoove these students to explore the best fit schools rather than those most favorably ranked.

About Sophie

Several years ago, Sophie and I sat down to revise her college list. During our discussion, Sophie hesitated as she pulled out a slightly wrinkled stack of paper, sloppily stapled and sprinkled with yellow highlighter. She told me that her mother had been researching psychology programs and had highlighted the ones to which Sophie should apply. It should come as no surprise that Sophie's mother had printed out the *US News & World Report*'s list of the best psychology programs, and it was this document that sat in front of us when we met. Sophie's mom had marked the "top ranked" and acceptable schools in highlighter. The trouble was (and the comedy of it never escapes me) that Sophie's mom had printed out a list of graduate psychology programs (and Sophie was in the eleventh grade!). And it should go without saying that at the very foundation of this story, Sophie's mom was doing the research—not Sophie. It is clear that Sophie's mother's reliance on this inappropriate list would have been foolish. Parents, acting like this is most certainly not demonstrating healthy parent involvement.

What Rankings Do Measure

Rankings lists are misleading in that they have little to do with measurement of actual student learning outcomes. Instead, they are influenced by a number of factors that many parents aren't even aware of. Rankings algorithms rely on schools' self-reported data, and that data can be manipulated or misrepresented. In other words, just because a college is moving up in the rankings does not necessarily mean that its student learning experience changed in any valuable way.

The undergraduate college rankings include fifteen metrics, each of which is assigned a weight by the *US News & World Report*; we will focus on some of the more problematic ones here. The reputation metric, called Expert Opinion, accounts for one-fifth of the formula. For this indicator, the publication asks presidents, deans of admission, and provosts, as well as a selection of high school counselors, to rate other institutions on a scale of one to five. Given the time these individuals spend working at their own institutions, they simply cannot be expected to know the nuances of hundreds of other institutions of higher education. What's more, some of these academic professionals concede that they have delegated the project to someone else in their office or simply haven't answered the survey. The reputation measure is a highly subjective measure that many experts purport is akin to a popularity contest.[1] Interestingly, if a college chooses not to participate in the rankings circus (there is a small percentage that does), the *US News & World Report* comes up with the missing data points on its own and the school's ranking inevitably falls considerably.[2]

How Colleges Can (and Do) Manipulate Rankings

Unfortunately for the students and families who blindly depend on and inappropriately revere them, rankings can be—and are—easily manipulated. In fact, several well-known institutions of higher education have copped to doing just that. Among them is Baylor, which in 2008 prodded its incoming class to retake SAT exams (to influence the standardized test metric), offering to reward the newly matriculated with a credit at the campus bookstore. Worse, they sweetened the deal by dangling a carrot in the form of $1,000 in student aid if that score increased by more than fifty points. And in 2012, news broke that Claremont McKenna College, one of five schools in the Claremont Colleges Consortium, had been falsifying its reporting of test scores for the previous six years in an effort to artificially increase its ranking.[3] How can *US News & World Report* even validate that the information they are collecting is legitimate?

The case of Northeastern University is perhaps one of the most drastic illustrations of the rankings manipulation "game." With an explicit goal to move considerably in the rankings, the school studied the rankings formula incessantly and made calculated changes that would result in a strategic rise on the *US News & World Report* list—and it worked. Over the course of ten years under then-President Freeland, who some call obsessed with drastically improving Northeastern's reputation via a significant move in the rankings, Northeastern University moved an astounding sixty-four spots![4]

The rankings system has also historically encouraged the byproduct of excessive marketing, and public relations agencies even help brand colleges to appeal to certain target applicant markets. The nonprofit testing companies The College Board and The ACT actually sell the names and addresses of students who have scores that fall into certain ranges to institutions that want to buy these names for their targeted mailings.[5] Colleges have learned that they can barrage all types of students with their marketing materials, encouraging as many students as possible to apply—even making those students who ultimately have no chance of admission to their institution feel as though they have a shot. Targeted personalized letters are mailed to thousands of students, making the less savvy consumers believe that they are in some way being identified by these schools as prime applicants. This practice increases the number of applications received while the number accepted remains constant—artificially increasing a college's selectivity.

It is worth noting that in 2018, the *US News & World Report* made some changes to its formula. These adjustments highlight what they call social mobility by recognizing those institutions that graduate Pell Grant recipients at high rates. (A Pell Grant is a type of grant from the federal government that is awarded to students based on their financial need, and it typically goes to students whose total household income is under $50,000 per year.) The adjustments also make an effort to deemphasize selectivity by omitting admission rates as a metric.[6]

What Rankings Do Not Measure

There are a host of characteristics that the rankings fail to measure. One of those important metrics is student debt. The relative student debt with which students graduate from an institution has no place in the algorithm—and with tuition ever increasing, this is a glaring omission.[7]

As Malcolm Gladwell points out in his compelling *New Yorker* piece on the fallacy of rankings, colleges' spending is regarded favorably when it comes to rankings—beautiful new buildings, higher faculty salaries—but alongside that increased spending come tuition increases. The competition among colleges that these rankings have perpetuated means that schools are spending more and more, building and growing, but it is the students who are footing the bill, graduating with more and more debt.[8] And no, unfortunately schools are not increasing their enrollment when these new dormitories and buildings are constructed.

Perhaps most importantly, though, rankings do not measure students' experiences; they do not look at whether a student can think critically, articulate, advocate, take initiative, serve, or manage by the time he graduates. They do not measure how well a school fits the student, how much hands-on experience he got, or what research tells us is another important factor in college success: the presence of mentors. Ted O'Neill, former Dean of College Admission at the University of Chicago, said it this way in a poignant speech on liberal arts education and college admission:

> How does our commitment to values lead to this deplorable situation? For a partial answer, we probably should

consider the influence of the *US News & World Report* college rankings. *US News* evaluates colleges, with a pretense to scientific precision, based on certain numbers. None of what they rate has to do with learning, or teaching, or the education of good people and good citizens.[9]

There's More to College Than the Name of the College

So what does this all mean? What should students and parents be thinking about during the college search and when they are choosing a school? Says one head of school confidentially:

> Here is what I say to parents regularly: There are more than fifteen great schools in the United States, and we've got to get over this obsession with name brand everything. It matters much more *what* you do in college rather than *where* you go. I feel we have all but ruined childhood because everything the kids do is high stakes now—sports are not for fun or fitness, but rather for getting recruited and then leveraging that to get into the best school possible . . . Every activity is in service of getting into the right college.[10]

Indeed, a very important white paper researched by Challenge Success in 2018 entitled *A 'Fit' Over Rankings: Why College Engagement Matters More Than Selectivity* examines the key factors that contribute to student outcomes and well-being beyond college. The report, which draws from current research, concludes that "college selectivity is not a reliable predictor of student learning, job satisfaction, or well-being." The results further indicate that "regardless of whether a student attends a college ranked in the top five percent or one ranked much lower, the research strongly suggests that engagement in college, how a student spends his or her time, matters much more in the long run than the college a student attends."[11]

During an interview with Dr. Michael Dennin, Vice Provost for Teaching and Learning at the University of California–Irvine, he, too, underlined the importance of examining fit during the college search process. "It is essential to understand that despite the national rankings out there, the rankings are really *not* relevant . . . The rankings do have some information," he continued, "but what is really important is to understand the type of school that best fits your child. Where will they thrive? Critical first questions are things like large versus small school, city versus suburb versus country, wide range of majors versus more focused school, and types of co-curricular activities (sports, orchestra, clubs, etc.)—as these can have a huge impact on the success of the student . . . Try to avoid a sense that there is one perfect school—as there never really is."[12]

The Power of Messaging and Biases

There's a common saying that rings true: *"College is a match to be made, not a prize to be won."* That quip has always stayed with me and has become a guiding principle in the work that I do with my students. It is our position as counselors that college rankings contribute much to the opposite of this principle. That is, rankings lend to the mindset that college is indeed a prize to be won and that a name on a list that is attached to a fickle number trumps any consideration of how a student will thrive when she sets foot on that campus. Colleges' desperate manipulations of the numbers only serves to fuel this madness and muddy the waters. It sends the message that the name is more important than the fit. Sadly, we see negative messaging damage the college admission process—and subsequently so many students' self-worth—all too often.

Consider Your Messaging

Where does that leave you? We challenge you to embrace the parent compass movement fully, putting the rankings aside (or at the very least, only using them as a jumping-off point to start exploring a variety of schools) and instead truly encouraging your high schooler to explore colleges that fit his learning style and goals.

But what this shift in perspective involves first and foremost is an examination of your messaging. Have you ever caught yourself assuring your teen that you will support him no matter where he gets into college, and then moments later enviously remark to a friend how impressed you are that Barbara's son was admitted to Princeton? Your child likely noticed you turning green. Or maybe you can cop to pushing your alma mater on your teen (or even just a school that you like) more than you would like to admit? What happens, then, when your son—try as he might—is not admitted to that school?

About Josh

A parent recently relayed to me a story that illustrates the biases we pass on to our children and just how acutely those biases affect them. Her son, Josh, was admitted to a college that by many accounts was a great fit for him. It had strong resources for his major, had the social environment that he was looking for, and it allowed him to have close interaction with his professors—an important component for this particular student. Josh was relaying the excitement of his acceptance to his friend while his friend's mother eavesdropped on the conversation. The friend's mother took but a few seconds to admonish Josh for his "ill-advised" enthusiasm, relaying her (ill-conceived) knowledge and inaccurate biases about the college in question. Dejected and embarrassed, and trusting that this adult surely knew better than he did, Josh decided not to attend this good-fit school.

Change Your Messaging

Parents, your kids (and their friends) listen even when you think they don't. Your comments impact them more than you think they do. What if you paid more attention to the messages that you are giving your children—whether intentional or not—as they relate to colleges you deem "acceptable" or "unacceptable," "highly ranked" or not? Dare to challenge your perceptions and look deeper. Here are some tips to help you change your messaging:

- Be willing to encourage your teen to search out schools that are the right fit for him or her, even if that means schools with which you are at first unfamiliar. We challenge you to visit college campuses in proximity to where you live and, if your financial situation allows, to visit those lesser known schools when you travel so that you can expose your teen to as many different types of campuses as possible. Learn firsthand about what each college can offer your child. Allow your teen to see what it is she is truly working toward, and be open to your teen's opinions—which may be different from yours.

- Avoid passing on your biases. You might think you know enough about a college to voice your opinion, but first ask yourself how much research you've really done. Are you an expert on what that school has to offer? Do you know any current students there, or is your opinion based only on what you knew a generation ago? How much do you know about its approach to educating students and the unique opportunities it offers?

- Do not do your child's college research for him. You are sending the message that he is incapable of learning in depth about the place at which he will potentially spend the next four years. What's more, it is during this research phase that students typically start to recognize what all of this work has been for. Instead, help your child understand how to peruse a college website and what he should be looking for, and then stand back and see what he finds. We recommend that he reads the online school newspaper to better understand the college's issues and news; takes a look at student organizations, clubs, and intramural sports that interest him; and checks out the course catalog and department website in his academic areas of interest.

- There is not one magical college that is the be-all end-all for your teen. We believe that there are multiple great-fit schools for your teen to explore, and that he will have the opportunity to thrive at any one of them.

- Invest in some earplugs—yes, really, do. Encourage your child to hold on to them as a reminder to be true to herself in this process and to trust her gut. Help her understand that she *can* tune out the noise to focus on what she believes to be the most fulfilling aspects of her college journey.

Alexandra Rhodes, a trusted colleague of ours, recently lamented the messaging that we are sending to this generation of tweens and teens when she noted:

"Stanford University admit rate falls to record-low 4.34 percent for class of 2023" is the headline. In other words, 96 percent of the hard-working, super-talented kids who applied to Stanford did not get accepted. We must stop making ten or twenty colleges such "prizes" because it's a lottery at this point, and if we continue to set up the validation for a child's hard work as admission to Stanford (or Harvard, Princeton, MIT, etc.), we are setting our kids up to fail. We have to make high school a place to learn, and the validation is learning. And then encourage our kids to go on to college, one of the [many] extraordinary four-year colleges in the US. We must open the pipeline of success beyond a few name-brand places that reject most of the qualified kids who apply because there simply aren't enough spots for them all (not because the kids have fallen short in any way).[13]

Recently, in anticipation of May 1 (the annual Decision Day and the deadline for students to deposit at the campus to which they plan to matriculate), we noticed a movement to bring positive messaging to the conversation around college choice. Rather than donning shirts emblazoned with their future institution's name, students at a high school in Illinois chose to label their own plain white shirts with handwritten messages of positivity: *My college does not define me* and *My choice = My happiness*.[14] This kind of messaging, we think, is refreshing and should be instructive to us all.

About Mallorie

Mallorie's two older siblings attended colleges that were more competitive than she desired. Mallorie was more of a middle-of-the-pack student and was also an artist and a dancer. I helped direct Mallorie to examine many colleges that were either off the beaten path or a bit less well known. Neither Mallorie nor her mom were familiar with many of the suggested schools, but my visits to them and experience with them told me they would be good-fit schools where Mallorie could chart a path of her own—one that didn't follow that of her siblings. Mallorie researched these suggestions; familiarized herself with the course and activity offerings, locations, and campus cultures; and talked to alumni and admission representatives. In the end, Mallorie applied to ten colleges across the country—and she was admitted to eight. Mallorie's confidence skyrocketed. She was even awarded merit aid and a spot on the dance team at a couple of them.

Mallorie's story is like many students who are academically situated somewhere in the middle. These kids are busy, mostly taking regular classes (not honors or AP), and most importantly share realistic college priorities with their parents. Mallorie's story is what we hope more and more stories look like for those who approach the college admission process with realistic expectations. *Knowing your child well, appreciating the person that he is, and helping him find a school fit that may be outside of a familiar list of well-known schools are important steps that follow the parent compass philosophy.*

Insert Your Earplugs

Those bright orange earplugs sure are a powerful tool. Ani said it best in an email to me during her freshman year of college: "I still have those earplugs you gave me," she wrote. "I know I absolutely wouldn't have gotten the opportunity [to be where I am] without having those earplugs in, just going for whatever I thought I'd like to do regardless of other opinions, so this is a real testament to how much your advice and mentorship is still helping me, past the college application process." We encourage you to join your child in employing these tiny devices and their noise canceling ability and to focus on what is best for *her* growth and development, *her* learning style and academic experience, regardless of what the chaos around you might be screaming in your ear.

CHAPTER 10:

BEHAVE DURING THE COLLEGE APPLICATION JOURNEY

The text came through at 4:05 AM. *Jason has shared a supplemental essay for your feedback.* Then another followed at 5:14 AM. *We are still confused about how to release test scores.* At 5:32 AM: *Should we use the Additional Information section essay we wrote to explain his sophomore grades?*

This smattering of texts was sent to me not by a student, but rather by one very overeager, overreaching, and over-involved parent. Let's put my mounting frustration aside for just a moment (and the not-so-pretty conversation I had to have with this mother about professionalism and appropriate involvement in her son's application process), and first address the use of the word "we" in this sample of text messages. "We are confused," "should we use," "we wrote" (the last one is the most alarming): parents, while your role is to support your student and offer feedback on college applications and essays, the pronoun "we" should be used infrequently. Now let's examine the other parts of this situation that were particularly disturbing. First, why was the mom rattling off these texts rather than her son? Second, why was she up at 4:00 AM and, if I'm reading in between the lines, seemingly doing some of the work for him? (No, she did not work in a profession that required her to be up in the middle of the night.) And third, when is it okay to text someone, professional or not, at 4:00 AM?

We understand that there are some blurry lines when it comes to supporting your child through the college admission process—how much do you plan, prod, push, proofread? Admittedly, it is a difficult place to settle into. You want your child to present the best version of herself, but let me ask you this: At what point does that version resemble you more than it does her?

So, what are the parent compass rules for navigating the college admission process? In this chapter, we will examine some of the most critical parts of the college admission process and provide some guidelines around when to get involved—and when to back off.

The College Search

Determining which colleges to apply to can be a daunting process. After all, there are over 4,000 of them to choose from. But that's just it: *there are over 4,000 colleges to choose from!* Parents, challenge yourself to approach the college search process with excitement for the exploration involved in learning about what's out there and with anticipation of uncovering something new, rather than limiting yourself to which small portion of those schools you'll "allow" your child to explore. You should be focused on helping your teen determine the right fit schools based on his unique academic needs and profile, personality, learning style, and social needs.

Help your child through the search process by providing resources. You can purchase a guidebook, or check one out from your local library, that your teen can flip through to see detailed descriptions of each school's standout academic programs, dorm life, surrounding environment, student culture, even quality of food. (Hint: our favorite is the *Fiske Guide to Colleges.*) What's more, many college guidebooks note "overlaps" for each school—other similar schools that might also interest a student. While your teen might think she has an idea of what type of school she wants, genuinely encourage her to explore other types of schools. We've found that not only do students' preferences change over the course of their college research (sometimes drastically), but also that they "don't know what they don't know." If they've never been exposed to a small campus and all of its benefits, how would they truly know whether or not they could thrive there?

The financial aspect of the college search is a complicated one and is one area wherein it is appropriate for you to take the lead, but we also feel that it is important to loop your child into the conversation. Setting limits and expectations from the beginning will help you avoid panic later in the process.

Campus Visits

If your financial situation permits you and your child to visit college campuses, navigate both the planning and execution of those visits with good parent etiquette. If, like many families, you are unable to travel for campus visits, we encourage you to explore virtual campus tours. Most colleges and universities feature these tours on their websites, and they can be a useful introduction to their campuses.

Planning

Determining the itinerary of your visits is something that you and your teen can do together. Really, it can be an intriguing puzzle trying to figure out how to visit multiple schools within just a few short days. While parents will usually need to take the wheel when it comes to booking flights if you're traveling far, there is no reason that teens cannot book tours and information sessions on each school's website. You can also encourage your teen to help research where to stay, if you will be traveling overnight. Many colleges have lists of nearby hotels on their websites, and often, discount codes are provided for prospective students. Teens who take part in the planning process feel as though they have some say in how the excursion unfolds and like they have some "skin in the game."

Execution

Students should prepare for their campus tours and information sessions beforehand. It can be helpful to arrive with some paper (or other note-taking device) and some carefully formulated questions to ask current students and admission officers. Parents, please let your child lead the way in asking questions. Empower him to approach admission officers to get the information that he needs. Encourage him to walk up to current students—chances are very high that he'll find a student who can't stop talking about the opportunities at the school. While you will likely have some "parent appropriate" questions to ask yourself, please don't overshadow your child. These campus visits are your child's chance at experiencing a glimpse of what college life will be like on certain campuses; it is not your time to show off the research that you've done, to annoyingly pepper the tour guide with questions your teen should be asking, or worse, to attempt to curry favor with an admission officer in the hopes that your teen will reap the benefits.

While visiting an East Coast campus with my own son, I was impressed that one college separated parents from their children and offered two distinct campus tours. If you think your teen would benefit more from touring without you, join in with another group or forego the tour altogether.

If you arrive to the campus only to encounter a rainy day or gloomy skies, or if your tour guide doesn't click with your teen, encourage her to look beyond any single impression as the basis of her judgment of the school. Just as a great teacher can make even the most boring material come to life and a dry teacher can "ruin" a teen's favorite subject, a campus tour is only a glimpse into a random day on campus. Both parents and students should maintain that perspective.

Personal Statements and Short Essays

About Lexi

It was the culmination of several months' work. Lexi had done a wonderful job working on an interesting personal statement that was both well-written and honestly portrayed who she was at the core. Curious and always inventing something new, Lexi gave the reader a glimpse into how her mind worked and the types of ideas that she generated on a daily basis. Proud of the work that she had put into this accurate reflection of who she was, she determined one day that her essay was complete. About a month later, Lexi asked me to skim over her essays prior to submission (there always seems to be an omitted comma or an incorrect homonym). I was startled when I reached her personal statement. Vastly different from her previous final draft, it used words and phrases that no high school student uses—much less those of us who actually attempt to write for a living. As she confessed that her mom had forced her to work with a writing tutor, her embarrassment was evident in her blushing cheeks. Taken aback, I was frank with Lexi: her authentic teen voice was gone and had been replaced by the verbose and sophisticated prose of an adult. The essay had, not surprisingly, lost its verve and playfulness. Lexi agreed and said that she would revert to its original version. But then I heard from Lexi's furious mom: How dare I accuse Lexi of cheating? (I did not.) How dare I assert that she did not participate in the process? (I did not.) While Lexi would amend the essay, her mother was clearly not pleased that this overly edited version would not be resting in the hands of admission officers.

Parents, your high schooler's personal statement, and all other application-related essays, should sound like they were written (or spoken) by—surprise—a high schooler. Some essays are incredibly well-written, some are a struggle to get through, just as some students are gifted with writing skills and some are not. The personal statement should read as though your teen is having a conversation with his reader. A general rule of thumb: if the essay was found on his high school campus with no name attached to it, would your teen's best friends or teachers know it was he who authored it and be able to recognize his distinct voice? They should by the tone and voice of the essay. Yes, essays need to be polished and thoughtful and they should probably go through more than one round of revisions, but every high school student applying to college is more than capable of "polished and thoughtful." Parents, check yourselves.

About Ethan

I most often received emails from Ethan during the middle of the school day. His language was business-like and professional as he frequently asked me to look over some of his essays and give him some feedback.

But you see, that's just it—they were too business-like and professional. As I dug into the attached essays, I came to realize that they were written (or over-edited) by Ethan's mom—and that the emails were coming from her, too. This was certainly a mom who used the pronoun "we" much too often in my interactions with her. After having a pointed conversation with Ethan and his mom, and educating them around the fact that admission officers are especially adept at determining when an essay is written or over-edited by a parent, the essays improved; Ethan came across less robotic and more like a real teenage kid with his own unique voice.

About Adina

When working with Adina one evening, she handed me a paper copy of her personal statement to read. She had completed it in seemingly record time. As I read her story, the vocabulary and style didn't seem to match the young woman I had come to know in our earlier sessions. When I asked her how she had crafted this essay so quickly and questioned if the content was indeed true, she was unembarrassed and stated, "I didn't write it. My mom did. And she did the same for my older sister who is now in college." I felt my cheeks redden, in shock at the matter-of-fact way in which she had shared that news with me. I couldn't ethically allow her to submit the essay, so I handed it back to her and asked her to come up with a story of her own—in her own voice. She sighed with discouragement, but in the end, she agreed and returned a few weeks later with a new draft that I knew she'd written. And guess what? It was so much better.

Parents, please realize that when your student earns a C in English but his essays read as though he were a regular contributor to the *New York Times*, your child is going to have a problem. You have not only quashed his voice but also shown him that you don't believe he has something special to say; you've told him that you can do it better and that you have a better understanding of what makes him tick than he does. And that behavior is, plain and simple, poor parent etiquette.

So, what is your role in the essay-writing process? You can help your teen recall memories and childhood anecdotes, participate in assisting her to identify her values, and talk to her about her strengths as you see them. Help her think through how she sees her strengths, and *ask her what she thinks her story is.* Ask questions and err more on the side of listening than talking. Generate ideas. But as you do, it is crucial to note the following: *What you think is defining about her might not be what she thinks best describes who she is. Have the courage to let it be. If you force a topic, it will likewise sound forced.*

About Anthony and Joey

Anthony was adopted, and his mother was certain that this fact alone comprised his story. She told me so multiple times. But when I asked Anthony about "his story," the fact that he was adopted didn't even find itself in our conversation. Eventually, after his mother had continually pressed on this topic, I asked him if he felt like adoption was the direction that his personal statement should go. He emphatically assured me that he would be staying away from the topic. His explanation? Yes, it was a part of him, but it didn't define him. To Anthony, his story could better be illuminated by highlighting his experiences camping and spending time in nature and how those times had shaped his perspective.

And then there was Joey. Joey's mom was adamant that her son write his personal statement about his experience in the Boy Scouts—and particularly about his Eagle Scout project. What's more, she wanted him to elaborate on other extracurricular activities in his essay (an approach that we do not recommend). She was incontrovertibly certain that this was what admission officers were looking for. But Joey had a different idea. You see, Joey loved trains. He vividly recalled the first time he had set eyes on one, then described his ensuing obsession that he quenched with books, shaky recordings of train rides, and trips to the local train depot. As time went on and his knowledge about trains grew, so did his fascination with transportation in general; eventually, he explored the inner workings of cars and airplanes and became intrigued by the field of engineering. However, unhappy with this topic idea, Joey's mom continued to push for her idea. Joey agreed to write two drafts: one addressing her topic and one addressing his. We'll give you one guess which one was more eloquent, from the heart, engaging, and descriptive of who he was. (And, to his mother's chagrin, was ultimately the one he submitted to colleges.)

Standardized Testing

It is a reality that many schools across the United States require standardized testing in the form of the ACT or the SAT as a condition for admission. As a parent, your role in this part of the college admission process should be *very* minimal.

If your teen struggles with test taking, you can help her explore the National Center for Fair and Open Testing (also known as FairTest at www.fairtest.org). This is an organization that seeks to expose the flaws of standardized testing and maintains an extensive list of schools that do not require standardized testing as part of the admission process (or that have flexible standardized test requirements).

Here are some ideas to help you navigate the maze of standardized testing:

- If your teen will be doing test prep on his own (i.e., studying without the help of a tutor), you can help by timing each section so that he doesn't have to rely on a cell phone or egg timer.

- If your teen will be working with a tutor or test prep company to prepare for the ACT or SAT, you can help research those in your area. But we encourage you to see what happens if your teen takes the lead in calling companies to gather information on tutoring style, pricing, and scheduling. After all, she is going to be the one to work with them. She can also ask if these companies offer free diagnostic practice tests in both the SAT and ACT so that she can see which test she prefers moving forward.

- Be realistic. Some teens are capable of scoring at the top end of the spectrum, while others aren't. Meet your child where he's at.

- Practice empathy. Let's face it: while in many cases standardized testing is a necessary byproduct of the college admission process, generally it isn't a fun one. Challenge yourself to refer to test prep and test taking from a place of compassion. Put yourself in your teen's shoes: Chances are you wouldn't find joy and deep fulfillment studying for such a lengthy exam either. Let your teen see that you understand and appreciate that she'd likely rather spend her time elsewhere.

Now, we hope you didn't think you were going to get away that easily. Here's where we tell you what not to do when it comes to standardized testing. Don't push and push—and push some more—for your child to continue to increase his score. We recommend sitting for no more than three exams, after which we often see test fatigue creep in and scores decline. And parents, it should go without saying: do not be tempted to make unethical mistakes like those you've seen play out in the media in Operation Varsity Blues.

Bad Application Behavior and Its Aftermath

Coincidentally, the first *Wall Street Journal* article about students' feelings toward their parents' involvement in the College Admissions Scandal emerged just as we were putting the finishing touches on this book. And while we intentionally chose not to focus on Operation Varsity Blues in this book, we nevertheless decided to reproduce the following manuscript as caution—to encourage our readers to pause and reflect on the excruciating ramifications of bad (and in this case, *really* bad) parent behavior. Readers, the heartache and regret that have resulted from parents who have crossed the line is palpable, and these mistakes have changed their families' lives forever:

Real Conversations from Operation Varsity Blues

The following quotes are directly from a *Wall Street Journal* article about the College Admissions Scandal:

"Why didn't you believe in me?" Matteo asked. "Why didn't you trust me?" . . .

"I never stopped believing in you, not even for one second," Mr. Sloane replied to his son that evening. "I lost sight of what was right, and I lost belief in myself." . . .

The Sloanes described intense parental anxieties about college that contributed to a pressure-cooker environment at home and school, an experience mirrored in accounts from many other families drawn into the scheme. . . .

Mr. Sloane saw himself in Matteo, his eldest, and had always told himself he would protect his son from any of the pain and disappointment he had felt. "This led me to try too vigorously to try to solve problems that hadn't yet arisen," Mr. Sloane said.

"From the ninth grade," Matteo said, "college counselors, moms, and dads [drill] a message into students: college, and a good one, [is] the goal. Parents [take] great pride—sometimes too much—in their children's accomplishments," he said.

"It's honestly, like, kind of gross that they're trying to live their kids' lives," Matteo said. "It doesn't give kids the breathing room they need to grow and develop into their own person." . . .

Meanwhile, Matteo was working furiously in school. "I grinded," he said. He'd come home from soccer practice or other extracurricular activities and then study until 2 a.m. some nights. He did a summer leadership program at Yale University. His parents would tell him how proud they were. . . .

"I failed miserably by doing too much, going too far, and crossing the line," [Mr. Sloane] wrote in a letter to the court.

And perhaps one of the most poignant parts of Matteo's experience is illustrated with these words:

"It kind of takes the value away of the work I did to get there in the first place," said Matteo, who took Advanced Placement classes, regularly made the honor roll his junior and senior years, and speaks three languages fluently. A few days before leaving for prison, Mr. Sloane said the worst part was knowing he hurt his eldest son. "By far," he said.[1]

The article continues to quote other parents embroiled in the scandal:

"I realize now that cheating on her behalf was not about helping her, it was about how it would make me feel" wrote Mr. Huneeus, now inmate No. 25453-111 . . .

at a California prison where he [served] five months. Since her father's arrest, [his daughter] has had panic attacks and worked with a psychiatrist.

Another indicted parent wrote to the judges: *"The lesson for me is to trust more in them, . . . [t]rust that they find their own path."* And another, *"I committed this crime for myself. Not because I wanted my son to go to any particular school, but because I needed to make myself feel like a better mother."*[2]

Parents, now that you have read these firsthand, painful accounts, we implore you: please do things differently.

Navigating Admission Decisions

Take a moment to picture your favorite roller coaster. Or, if you aren't a Space Mountain or Kingda Ka fan, consider the scariest roller coaster you can conjure up. There are high peaks and low valleys, twists and loops, moments where you feel like your stomach is going to be sick and others where you couldn't be more excited, and moments where you're shaking and moments where you can't quite think straight. Parents, this topsy-turvy description also illustrates the college admission decisions experience. Your child will encounter a roller coaster of emotions, starting at joy and relief, cresting at deep sadness, and then circling back through it all once again (and possibly again and again). And *you* will likely experience these emotions right alongside her. Please, we implore you: talk about college decisions early—before they are released. Prepare your child; don't wait until the decision letters come to broach the subject.

Navigating Unfavorable Decisions

Fellow parents, let me break it down for you. *Failure is virtually an inevitable part of this process.* And we know it's no fun to embrace, but it is the truth. Your child will almost certainly experience heartache, disappointment, anger, and defeat. He will cry, and you will cry. In our experience, even when students and families swear up and down that they are ready to accept disappointment and even when families tell us that they understand failure is a necessary evil inherent in this process, many families still hope and wish and dream; they hold on to the possibility that disappointment won't actually come knocking at their door. While it's fine to hope and dream, parents also need to prepare their children through real conversations about disappointment—about moving through the pain to focus on the joy.

We all have days when something really bad happens. Think about that day when you made a mistake, or maybe someone at work yelled at you, or perhaps you got into a fender bender. Why is it so much easier to focus on that one bad thing and completely discount the other fourteen wonderful things that happened that very same day? The man who smiled at you, the woman who purchased your coffee because you forgot your wallet in the car (yes, that's happened to me), the person who paid your parking meter just as it ran out of time, your child telling you out of the blue that he appreciates something that you do: Why do we tend to allow the bad to overshadow the good?

We think that this same concept goes for the admission decisions process. Help your child to focus on the good in the process. Maybe she was admitted to six schools and wasn't admitted to two; help her to focus on those six rather than dwell on those two.

We'd also like to take a moment to address the word "reject." Almost unfailingly, when a student calls or emails us to pass along an admission decision and the decision was not positive, he reports that he was "rejected." In fact, most schools use the terminology "denied admission," but somehow, the word "rejected" has wormed its way into almost universal use when referring to an unfavorable admission decision. You'll notice, however, that nowhere in this chapter have we used that word. The verb form of *reject* means "to dismiss as inadequate, inappropriate, or not to one's taste." Parents, when did college admission come to define (and become so intricately tied to) our children's self-worth? When did it become a vehicle for telling our kids that they are inadequate, inappropriate, or not to taste? The reality is that, sure, they were not admitted to a school—they were *denied admission*—but we challenge you to think about terminology here. Encourage your child to loosen the tie to what he *thinks* an unfavorable decision might mean about him as a person; help him to see it as what it is: a hope that didn't work out and instead can be an opportunity to practice resilience.

Finally, consider what this former school headmaster had to say about admission results that were not what students or their parents hoped for: "[P]arents often had no faith in their children's resilience. The kids generally survived rejection from their dream schools better than their parents."[3]

Navigating Favorable Decisions

So, your daughter was admitted? Jump up and down. Do a dance with her. Scream, cry, laugh, hug. But, fellow parents, please behave. Go ahead and tell family and close friends, but we urge you to wait until you calm down. Remember that your friends are likely experiencing the roller coaster detailed above. Resist the urge to post the play-by-play all over social media. No one likes a braggart.

An enthusiastic parent recently posted a video recording on social media depicting her child screaming and crying with joy over a college acceptance. But when her son arrived at school the next day, not only did his friends tease him, but worse, they shut him out. Classmates (and their parents) are not always genuinely happy for their peers. Please, understand that this is a very precarious and sensitive time for teens and their families. Show some restraint and decorum. We share this story with you to serve as a wake-up call and warning. And we implore you: don't be that parent.

To conclude this chapter, we offer a silver lining—an example of parents learning from their children. In Palo Alto, California, at a large public high school located across the street from Stanford University, a group of students decided to take a stand and combat the ultra-competitive nature of their community; they decided to fight against the alarming numbers of teen suicides that had cropped up in their community. "The student newspaper's top editors decided to scrap the who's-going-where college map amid growing worries it was feeding an unhealthy culture obsessed with success." Other schools around the country have also taken similar stands. One local parent who attended Palo Alto High School a generation ago reflected that "back then" this edition of the paper was not that big a deal but that now, "It's gotten more intense . . . People tend to treat their kids like pets in a pet show." This student decision to "scrap the map" demonstrates hope for the future, as it aims to combat a "toxic, comparison-driven culture."[4] A published college list truly doesn't define the success of each student.

We agree with these wise words from a parent: "We need a change in how high schools approach college [admission]. When their students are admitted to elite colleges, almost every high school will be sure to get the word out (at graduations, senior awards ceremonies, etc.). Until high schools stop touting [admission] to specific schools as a barometer of academic or other achievement (and a measure of their own success as teachers and administrators), we can't expect attitudes to change."[5] Fellow parents, be that change in attitude that your community—and your child—needs.

CHAPTER 11:

RECOGNIZE MOST THINGS ARE NOT CATASTROPHIC

Jessie clicked her mouse to bring up the admission decision. Subconsciously holding her breath and clenching her hands together, she slowly realized that the words she desperately didn't want to encounter were, in fact, staring back at her from her computer screen. She didn't know whether to cry or to scream, so naturally, she did both. Jessie was a complete and utter failure—well, at least that's what she thought.

Jessie's mother contacted me in anguish when her concern for her daughter grew. Jessie didn't seem to be handling this admission decision well. After all, she had put so much time and effort into her applications—not to mention into her classes and tests, activities, and athletics throughout her four years of high school. But Jessie had been accepted to seven other schools, and her concerned mother didn't understand why Jessie could only focus on the negative outcome and the destructive thought that it made her a complete failure.

Parents, remember back to when you were trying to teach your child to write his name or to ride his bike. As any parent knows, eventually children get it, but the process can involve great frustration and tedium. You might have even heard a very dramatic, "I am *never* going to be able to do this," along the way. The truth is, kids of all ages often fall prey to errors in their thinking, and an inaccurate perception of reality can result in a negative view of the world. One error might generalize to a completely doomed future, or one unintentional slight by a friend might translate into an assumption that a particular friendship is over. Teenagers can tend to see inconveniences and setbacks as catastrophes from which recovery is unlikely or, worse, impossible. Parents riddled with anxiety can catastrophize, too. Have you ever caught yourself compulsively playing out the worst-case scenario? Maybe your infant started walking later than his peers and—fast-forward—you pictured him crawling to his first day of junior high. And then in junior high, when he had a bad semester, you pictured him jobless and living in a ditch somewhere. Parents, your job is to recognize and subsequently help your teen through these damaging thinking patterns—and to keep your own distorted thoughts in check, too. Following the parent compass should help curtail your own anxieties spilling over to your child.

Helping Teens Who Catastrophize

With tweens and teens in the house, most days probably feel like a catastrophe has taken place: a friend of your daughter shared an unflattering photo of her on social media (the world is ending!), meatloaf was served for dinner instead of tacos (the nerve!), or everyone *else's* parents let them use their phones during homework time (how could one survive?!). But catastrophizing can be a very real thing and a legitimate (although rather illogical) feeling for your teen. Have you ever heard the saying, "anxiety lies in the future, not in the present"? When your child spends too much time thinking in grand terms about what may (or in this case, will likely not) happen in her future, it can rob her of the joy of remaining present in the moment.

When your student receives a C on one test and remarks that he is a terrible student or when he doesn't have his best water polo game and concludes that he is the team's worst player and he might as well quit, be on high alert; this pattern of thinking is dangerous, because students can use it as an excuse to throw in the towel. In fact, it is the opposite of the grit and resilience that we've been advocating throughout this entire book. As discussed in Chapter 3, grit and resilience arise from, in part, doing difficult things—in stretching oneself, in picking up and gathering oneself after a setback, and in taking up the challenge to try again or to try a different way. Yet teens who are constantly stuck in the "But what if . . . ?" of life instead feel paralyzed into inaction.

About Adriana

I remember meeting Adriana a few years back when she was diligently preparing for the ACT. She spent hours working through test prep books and devoted her Saturdays to taking practice exams, on which she scored quite well. During her studying and as she nervously awaited the official test day, she articulated to me that she was proud of her effort. When that ill-fated Saturday came, Adriana sat to take the exam and left the testing center feeling generally confident in her performance. Several weeks later, though, Adriana received her score, and it was not nearly what she had hoped it would be. To say that Adriana took the news hard is an understatement. Devastated, she dubbed herself "a horrible test taker" and told me that she wasn't capable of scoring well (despite evidence to the contrary on her practice exams). Adriana mistakenly assumed that she was simply unable to earn her goal score—all based on one poor performance on one particular Saturday in October. To her, it wasn't worth taking the test again, because she was just going to keep scoring poorly.

About Connor

I remember when Connor earned a B in first semester physics. Mostly an A student, Connor was beside himself with grief over this "transgression." You see, Connor took this B and magnified it to epic proportions, playing the B out over time and ultimately coming up with the conclusion that he was not going to get into college—anywhere! Connor's mom called me in a panic, wondering if his assessment was accurate. The answer was a hard no. But this type of thinking takes a toll on a student's self-esteem; parents should first point out, listen to, and acknowledge the feelings their teen is having, and then help him to remedy it by using the strategies outlined later in this chapter.

Focusing on the Negative

I see it happen all the time: students who simply ignore an abundance of positives only to focus on one negative. And it always seems to happen a lot around the time that admission decisions are sent (remember Jessie, whom we met at the outset of this chapter?). But when your teen focuses on the negative to the detriment of the abundance of positives constantly surrounding her, it does her no good; in fact, it keeps her swimming in a pool of harmful thoughts rather than experiencing the true joy in the positive aspects of her life (and no matter who you are, there are always positives to be identified each and every day).

If you find that your tween or teen is focusing on the negative—discounting the positives in a particular situation or even more generally in his day to day—try this exercise: encourage him to make a "positives" list. You can even sit with him while he does the activity, if he'll let you. Have him write out all of the good things that came alongside the negative situation on which he is focusing. Urge him to habitually review his list and add to it. You can point out the positives that you see as well.

In a related activity, you can help your teen focus on the things for which he is grateful. Constantly paying homage to the abundance of things that bring us joy keeps our focus on the good rather than the bad. Let's face it: we are confronted with challenges each and every day, but when we actively work to concentrate on the good, no matter how small, the more likely we are to experience a greater sense of well-being. In our house, we each name one thing from the day that we are grateful for before we go to bed each night. It can be as simple as the delicious latte I enjoyed with my breakfast or the fact that I made it to the pharmacy two minutes before it closed. Some people choose to keep gratitude journals that they add to periodically or even daily, which helps them to track the good things in their life over time and to naturally dwell on the positive.

Yet another strategy is to ask your teen how she would perceive her situation if it had happened to a stranger. If someone at another school, for instance, got a B for one semester of physics, would that mean that she wasn't admissible to college? Your teen's perception may change quickly when a stranger is experiencing the situation, and the exercise depersonalizes it for your teen.

Parents, don't be afraid to point out your teen's maladaptive thinking to him; listen, show empathy, and ask some general questions to help redirect his thinking so that eventually, he can catch himself before he makes the error in judgment. For instance, Adriana had completed multiple practice tests on which she had earned her goal score or above. Adriana's parent might sit down with her and take a look back at those practice test scores, showing her physical proof that she is capable of meeting her goal score.

You can also try something a little bit more elaborate that takes some creative on-the-spot thinking and play a game with your tween or teen, putting the irrational thought on "trial." The "defense" will outline its case, offering the supporting evidence for the assumption that your teen would fail all subsequent tests (or whatever her negative thoughts are focused around). The "prosecution" would provide evidence to the contrary, attempting to prove that the thought is irrational. Once both sides have presented their cases, the "judge" (your teen) gets to decide whose case was more compelling.[1]

Recognize Catastrophizing in Yourself

I used one particular example at the start of this chapter not by accident. You see, I *was* the parent whose child walked later than my friends' kids did, and I quite literally had irrational visions of her crawling to her first day of class in junior high. Never mind that the pediatrician told me that it was actually good for her development to crawl and that she wasn't actually late at all; the *other kids* were all walking—no, running—while I waited quite impatiently. And now, years later, just as the doctor told me, she is developmentally where she needs to be. Parents, how many of you can relate to playing out a relatively simple situation or worry only to end up in the very worst place? It's a normal thing to do, and in our competitive world, we constantly feel the need to keep up with the Joneses. But what if we took that ball of anxiety and just placed it, instead, into having a heap more faith in our kids? Why couldn't I trust my daughter to walk when she was ready? Because that's exactly what she did. Well, probably because I was too worried with how it might reflect on me. And this is where we come full circle: Remember the self-assessment that you took at the very start of this book? Thinking the worst, living in a future that likely won't materialize, is robbing you of the joy of experiencing the present journey with your child.

Life Isn't Always Fair

"But it's just not fair." This is something I often hear at my desk. It's not fair that he won the award and I didn't; it's not fair that the teacher likes her better; it's not fair that her parents help her and mine don't; it's not fair that I have to get a job. But let's review what probably every one of our parents told us, and indeed we all likely tell our own kids: life's not fair. Holding ever so tightly to the belief that it is will only lead to a constant sense of dissatisfaction and unnecessary comparison.

I think the time that I hear most about fairness (or, really, unfairness) is when students receive admission decisions; that's what is most pertinent to our conversation here. And the reality is that, yes, the admission process is inherently not fair. Students with lower GPAs might be admitted over him, athletes or legacy students might be given preferential treatment over him, an unkind bully might be admitted when he wasn't, a cheating incident might be concealed from or overlooked by admission officers—all of these things and so many more might be perceived as unfair, and they might very well be, but we live in an unfair world. But a student who holds steadfastly to the idea that things should and must be fair—especially in the world of college admission—is going to find himself angry and sorely disappointed, time and time again.

Long before applications are even completed and certainly well before decisions have come out, initiate frank conversations with your teen about the idea of fairness and how to cope in school, in life, and in college admission when things aren't fair. Give him situations from your life that have been unfair, and tell him how you have coped. Passed over for a work promotion? Lost a job to someone younger than you? Had to move your family to a new city just when your kids had finally found their groove from the most recent job transfer? Remind your teen that you, too, have experienced unfair life experiences, but that you have come out of them stronger, more resilient, and, yes, sometimes still with a small grudge over what should be let go as ancient history. Life is not easy and not always fair. Then, try to work through unfair hypothetical scenarios and challenge your teen to come up with ways to cope with the disappointment and anger. What happens when you lead the group project and everyone gets the same grade—even the kid who didn't do anything? How would you move on if a classmate with lower grades and test scores was admitted to a school and you were not? Fellow parents, it is not, "What an injustice! I assure you, I will fix this." Instead, say, "Honey, I will sit with you through this disappointment, and we will work to focus on the positive." Practice those situations long before they happen. And listen. And show empathy. And ask some open-ended questions—all before trying to help solve or fix any of your teen's feelings for him.

Constructing a Script as You Navigate

Working from a script, when we are first attempting to grasp a concept or practice a habit, can help give us a useful roadmap. We've come up with a few sample scenarios to illustrate appropriate responses to perceived "life isn't fair" scenarios, and to juxtapose those responses with inappropriate ones.

THE SCENARIO: *Ana, your daughter's teammate, got to start in the volleyball game despite the fact that she missed two practices this week. Your daughter is furious; she made every practice, but since Ana is a better player, she still gets to start.*

Inappropriate Response: "What? There is no way she should start while *you* sit on the bench. The athletic director will be hearing about this!"

Appropriate Response: "Your frustration is natural. I totally get it. Accepting life's inequities never gets easy, but you just keep doing your thing the right way and hopefully you will get recognized for your effort. After all, you love volleyball. Keep hanging in there."

THE SCENARIO: *JT, a student in your son's grade, was accepted to a certain college, but your son was not, despite his better grades (or at least that's what your son thinks).*

Inappropriate Response: "This is absolutely ridiculous. You have worked too hard for JT to get in over you. Jeanette said his SAT score was at least twenty points lower than yours. There has to be a mistake, and we are going to fix this. I will call the school counselor in the morning."

Appropriate Response: "Gosh, I understand how that might make you feel. It's really hard when things don't work out the way we envision them to. But let's choose to focus on the schools that are really excited at the prospect of you becoming a student."

THE SCENARIO: *Erica, whose mom is the school's volunteer "theater mom," always gets the larger parts in the school shows. She's not a very strong singer, and she's also very braggy about the roles that she gets. Your own daughter has been passed over yet again, despite her stronger singing voice, kinder attitude, and dance experience.*

Inappropriate Response: "Time and again the theater director gives the leads to the volunteer mom's daughter. I swear, he picks favorites. How unfair! And Erica is so unkind to the other castmates and never remembers her blocking or lines. He is so swayed by and afraid of this powerful mom."

Appropriate Response: "I totally get it. This is terribly frustrating. I remember the same thing happened to me in middle school, over and over again. There is always going to be 'an Erica and her mom.' Stay the course, show up on time, know your lines, be patient. Let's talk about what you *can* do and what *is* in your control."

The anxiety and hopelessness that can result from a negative view of reality will only add to the already difficult teen and tween years. Parents should be aware of the dangers of catastrophizing life events—both in teens and in themselves. This awareness will help in finding and discussing solutions to help their teens restructure their thinking to align more with reality.

CHAPTER 12:
BE OPEN TO ALTERNATIVE ROUTES

Jared was determined to become a professional ballet dancer; the dancing bug bit him "late" in the game—after he was required to take a ballet class for his high school musical, *A Chorus Line*, when he was in tenth grade. Jared first showed up to his ballet classes begrudgingly, but he quickly discovered that he had a natural talent to leap, lift, and turn. He became intrigued by ballet and decided to enroll at a local ballet studio when *A Chorus Line* ended. Less than a month later, Jared was dancing six days a week and was cast as the lead in the spring ballet performance. He was also accepted to a summer ballet intensive on the other side of the country. After dancing all summer, Jared realized he wanted ballet to be more than just an after-school activity.

Once Jared learned that there is a peak success time for male ballet dancers, he didn't want to miss his window of opportunity; he wanted to pursue his newfound passion full force. While he had always been a serious student, he knew that attending his college-prep high school would not allow him the training time he needed. After some coaxing via painting a logical argument of how well he had thought through his future divergence, he convinced his (open-minded) mom to support his decision to pursue a professional career in ballet. But this meant attending a more rigorous ballet program in another city and taking a different approach to his junior and senior years. He enrolled in online courses and local community college classes as a "dual-enrolled" high school student, meaning he concurrently earned both high school and college credit. He spent close to four hours a day commuting by bus to his new studio—seven days a week—and he worked tirelessly to make up for lost time. He also got a job at a local coffee shop to help cover transportation costs. This windy path led him to discover his dream of being accepted into a professional ballet trainee program, and with his mom's support and the flexibility of community college, he was able to make it work. We applaud the parenting etiquette that Jared's mom exhibited. She was willing to support her son's interest—even if it meant veering from a direct path and traditional college route.

Not all teens blossom or mature at the same time and in the same way, and sometimes, life presents its roller-coaster twists and unexpected turns. While some students peak in high school, others don't peak until well after it is over, when they have had a chance to grow up outside of their childhood homes and apart from their involved parents. We can all attest to the fact that life's route from point A to point B is rarely a straight or direct line; ask anyone who has "arrived" at an academic or professional destination, and they will likely tell you that their journey tended to be indirect, curvy, and circuitous. The good news is that nowadays there are many alternatives to the traditional college route, which will be explored in this chapter. Parents, try to be open to these alternatives and whether or not they are the appropriate choice for your child; don't remain stubbornly stuck on your hopes for a more traditional path that simply does not fit him.

The Gap Year

"My teen is taking a gap year." Ten years ago: a gasp. Sure, gap years used to be secret code for "My kid isn't ready for college," or, "My teen really needs some time to mature." It was utilized by kids who didn't do very well in high school and needed to get a restart or teens who wanted to build some life experience and "better" their academic coursework results in order to reapply to college. But today we are seeing a shift. While a proclamation that your kid is taking a gap year might not always be met with supportive curiosity, we do, in fact, see an increasing number of parents who applaud the choice of extra breathing space. It is now often seen as an opportunity for maturity coupled with time off of the academic grind—a time to allow teens to gain clarity and some idea of personal direction and focus.

And yes, there are still parents reluctant to go off of the beaten path, afraid that this less traditional route might somehow limit or harm their children. To those parents: we encourage you to be flexible. Observe this as an *opportunity* instead of a limitation for your high school graduate. Gap years can be the perfect antidote to burnout or college acceptance disappointment, among other things. With big businesses offering internships and outdoor education opportunities, gap year programs even provide some employment experience for new high school graduates. Embrace the gap year, *if that's what's right for your child.* Encourage your son or daughter to still apply to colleges as a high school senior, as it is easiest to apply then due to internal support from high school counselors and teachers. Once decisions arrive, in many cases, your teen can contact the college to request that her start date be deferred for a year, enabling her to pursue a gap year. Conversely, if the goal of the gap year is to create more college opportunities, then by all means apply again a year later to see if there will be more options after the gap year experience.

About Jordan

Jordan was in the middle of his class academically, completed an AP or honors class annually, participated on an athletic team, served a bit of community service, and was a part-time employee in the summer. But he was showing incredible signs of wear and burnout by the start of his junior year; he wasn't even sure he wanted to apply to college. And he, his parents, and I all noticed it, as did his teachers and school counselor. Something had to change. When I introduced him to the idea of a gap year directly after high school, he was convinced that his parents wouldn't go for it. But I thought otherwise. A quick phone call with Jordan's mom and dad introduced them to this alternative route, and they subsequently met with the school counselor. Everyone agreed to get on board with the idea—for the sake of preserving Jordan's mental health and high school sanity. Just the promise of a year off after high school was enough of a motivator for Jordan to push through the four-year grind and graduate from high school emotionally intact. He set realistic college goals at good-fit schools, since I had advised him to apply to college right out of high school and then defer a year (instead of trying to find the motivation to reapply after spending six to nine months clearing his head in the real world). After a year of combined travel, work, and some study, Jordan returned to college one year after his classmates—but now he was recharged and renewed, proof that the gap year had been the right choice for him. And lucky for Jordan, when his parents saw the results of his choice in plain sight, they were glad to have gotten on board.

Internships and Travel

Internships and travel can be done either before, during, or after college. Interning for a professor, doctor, or other professional businessperson is a great way for your high school graduate to gain some "real-world" experience and career exposure. Many students or pre-professionals complain that it is hard to get a job without experience, and it is hard to get experience without a job! As a parent this could be a helpful time for you to network with other adults in order to assist your teens in making connections. Following your parent compass certainly allows room for parent networking and introductions to help open some doors for your teen (just not getting a job for your teen and outright nepotism). Your teen needs to experience the application and interview process and earn the experience beyond the initial connection. Some students seeking internships resist the idea of family connections, but truly these connections simply open a small door for applicants; your teen still has to interview, apply, and win the position. While it is never a good idea for a teen to intern for a business that shares the same last name as yours or one at which you work, it is fine to make introductions with colleagues, friends, and relatives. Lucky for your teen, internships are not always difficult to obtain, as your teen is offering free assistance and a willingness to do menial tasks for anyone who wants help! And we all have to start somewhere. You can also offer your expertise toward your friends' or co-workers' kids in the form of an internship or even a job shadow, if there is a student that expresses an interest in learning more about your profession. Remember, following your parent compass allows door opening—just not pushing too hard.

Travel on either a Eurail Pass, around-the-world flight ticket, or through working as a teacher or nanny in a foreign country are more ways for students to gain exposure and experience in other cultures, with other languages, and with different customs. Travel can also get your teen out of her local bubble. Living, working, traveling, volunteering, or studying abroad is also a popular post-collegiate activity worth exploring. Whether with a national organization (like Plan My Gap Year, Projects Abroad, Abroadly, Global Leadership Adventures, Birthright, or Semester Abroad) or on her own, there are scores of programs and opportunities that your teen can research to afford her a more global experience. (For more opportunities and programs, see the Appendix.)

Starting College One Term In

Many colleges admit new freshmen but defer them until the spring term. They encourage these new students to either participate in an overseas campus affiliated with the college during that first term, take approved semester-long classes at their local community colleges for transfer credit, or simply delay their arrival and fill the time how they choose. This mid-year delayed college arrival is not uncommon, and colleges choose to do this for a variety of reasons—both economical and logistical (to scatter freshman start times among other things).

About Beth

Beth was admitted to a college program wherein she started in the fall at the university's London program before heading back to the States for the second half of her freshman year and the rest of college. At first, she was disappointed at the thought of starting at the main campus later than her peers and in a non-traditional way, perhaps missing out on those exciting first days of bonding through school spirit and a new-found sense of freedom. Looking back on the experience, however, she was thrilled to have had it. She recalls: "I created amazing overseas memories in a dorm with thirty other classmates from all over the world with whom I could share these special memories. It was the best of both worlds for me. I got to basically build deeper relationships with these new people in an overseas setting. I wouldn't change the way this worked out for me in any way." Her parents were admittedly perplexed and disappointed for their daughter at the outset, but they tried to put on a positive face and support this alternative start date. However, as they helped Beth move into her on-campus dorm for the second semester of her freshman year, their daughter's increased open-mindedness and self-confidence as a result of living abroad put them at ease. Parents, be flexible and accept alternative choices, views, and routes to those you may have taken a generation ago.

Community College

About Jackie

Jackie was determined to leave her home state of Texas to attend college in California. At just eighteen years old, she did not have financial support from her parents. Jackie had been saving up to realize her dream—since the young age of twelve—babysitting all over town. She found a job as a live-in nanny in California for a large family, packed up her car with all of her belongings, and drove herself to the Golden State. Jackie enrolled at a local community college, but unfortunately she ran into a snag: she was not yet a resident of California, so she was forced to pay out-of-state fees for her classes. But, Jackie pushed ahead—using all of her earnings to put herself through school—persevered, and eventually earned the grades to transfer into a university. Upon graduation, she landed her lifelong dream job as a wedding planner and moved to Las

Vegas, where she has coordinated over 400 weddings to help others find their happily ever afters—just as she did.

About Anne

At seventeen years old, Anne was in a terrible car accident. A distracted driver had run a red light, slamming into the rear of the driver's side—exactly where Anne was sitting. Her memories of that night were minimal: flashing lights, weeping, voices that she couldn't quite place. In the months that followed, Anne slowly rehabilitated, attending weekly physical therapy appointments, therapy for the trauma, and doctor's appointments to monitor her slow progress. She often missed school to work these necessities into her day. But what took her out of school the most were the headaches. Anne had endured a serious concussion, resulting in debilitating headaches that typically occurred just a few hours into the school day. Unable to concentrate, she'd shuffle to the nurse's office and wait for her mother to pick her up.

Not surprisingly, Anne's grades suffered her junior year. A standout student before the accident, Anne struggled as she fell behind in every one of her classes. While she had accommodations, the incompletes piled up. Junior year bled into senior year, and Anne still hadn't completed her eleventh-grade work well into the fall of twelfth grade—and all the while the headaches continued. It became clear that Anne needed to explore alternative options, giving herself time to heal before heading straight into a four-year university.

There are an abundance of reasons that going to community college makes sense for students in lieu of going right into a four-year university. Sometimes a teen simply needs better grades or proof that he can hack it in a classroom—better than he did in high school. Other times, the high cost of college prohibits students from starting a four-year college right out of high school, and community college provides an affordable way to rack up transfer credits to bring into college as a transfer student. And sometimes, like in Anne's case, life just happens. Many community colleges even have transfer admission guarantee (TAG) programs with their state colleges. (Check if your state has TAG programs or the equivalent, or research the university you hope to attend so that you are sure to take courses that will transfer seamlessly for credit.)

Reasons to Attend Community College

1. Cost-effective courses to transfer to four-year college

2. Get general education requirements out of the way

3. Need to help at home by working, supporting a family member in need, or caring for siblings

4. Need to get some better grades slated than received in high school (late bloomer)

5. Want to improve odds to transfer into a four-year college

6. Need a flexible schedule to allow for work and study

7. Need to live at home for personal, health, or financial reasons

8. Want an option that is convenient and local

Career Colleges or Apprenticeships

Author, producer, and television host of Discovery Channel's *Dirty Jobs* and CNN's *Somebody's Gotta Do It*, Mike Rowe is outspoken on his support of alternative paths instead of college. He says, "I think a trillion dollars of student loans and a massive skills gap are precisely what happens to a society that actively promotes one form of education as the best course for the most people. I think the stigmas and stereotypes that keep so many people from pursuing a truly useful skill, begin with the mistaken belief that a four-year degree is somehow superior to all other forms of learning."[1]

If your teen does not want to take a traditional academic route to college and prefers to learn a skill that can be immediately productive in the marketplace, then a career college may be worth exploring. Career colleges provide pre-professional training and a license or certification in areas such as medical billing and coding, veterinary technology, health care, interior design, cosmetology, and hospitality, among other things. These privately owned, for-profit colleges prepare students for careers through a relevant, intensive curriculum. Unlike community colleges, where students take courses in multiple disciplines, career colleges usually focus on a main area of expertise that a student is trying to gain. Some do require academic courses, for example in English or history, while others relate every class to a specific job, business, or technical field. Your teen may want to study to become an Emergency Medical Technician (EMT), to begin a career in law enforcement, or to pursue firefighting. If accepted into those programs, students sometimes can get paid while training.

An apprenticeship, on the other hand, is a working relationship between a worker and employer where the employee learns a skilled trade through classroom work and on-the-job training. Apprenticeship programs can last anywhere from several months to a year or more. A person completing an apprenticeship generally becomes a skilled craftsperson in a particular trade. For example, some students like working with their hands and have the skill, patience, and temperament to become expert mechanics, carpenters, or electronics repair technicians. If your teen expresses interest in one of these professions and feels that traditional college isn't for him (or that it isn't for the time being), then explore the idea of an apprenticeship. Visit the Department of Labor's Office of Apprenticeship website for more information.

Joining the United States Military

What if your teen wants to work for the largest employer in the country? If your family has a history of relatives who have served in the military, then this is familiar territory and might be a less complicated choice for your teen. On the other hand, if military service is an unexplored career possibility for your teen, you will all have some homework to do through researching, asking questions of those who have served, and visiting a local military base. Once your teen has determined that the military is an avenue she wants to pursue, she has to determine which branch is right. Also, your teen should consider the following factors: length of enlistment, advanced pay grade, additional pay and allowances, and the ability to pursue higher education while serving or at the end of service. If your teen chooses to continue with processing for enlistment, she will need to take the Armed Services Vocational Aptitude Battery (ASVAB).[2]

Straight into the Workforce

Some students skip college altogether and go right into the workforce; we often hear stories of successful working college dropouts or those ready to go right into the working world with their skills and talents. Sometimes workforce jobs begin with paid or unpaid internships, where teens and young twenty-somethings start at the very bottom (in the mailroom, running coffee, or being a task rabbit) and the on-the-job training leads to more permanent entry-level positions. We have read news articles about many dropouts who go on to do great things without completing their college degrees; some have become celebrities such as Mark Zuckerberg, Steve Jobs, and Bill Gates. Others are in entertainment, like Ellen DeGeneres, Brad Pitt, or Oprah Winfrey. But many lesser known students have left school to pursue their passions or purposes. Dropping out of school takes courage and is not the straightest path to a traditional career: "More often than not, a successful college dropout is the exception and not the rule. The majority of America's roughly 34 million college dropouts are more likely to be unemployed, in debt, defaulting on their loans, and impoverished."[3] So, we are not necessarily recommending going straight into the workforce, here, but we do want to point out that—of course—some students do choose to forego college or drop out after attending for a period of time in order to join the workforce sooner.

Q: My son didn't do well in high school academically, made less-than-stellar impressions on his teachers, and really didn't care about high school. His friends are getting college acceptances and he is not. Is it better for him to take a gap year or to attend community college and then try to transfer? Or try to get a menial job?

A: *Not all teens bloom at the same time, as you may have just discovered through personal experience! Attending community college is a great way to boost confidence, get on track academically, and take general education requirements. It's also an affordable alternative to college. Community colleges also serve as excellent pathways into four-year universities. A gap year is also a great choice for students who need to press the pause button, take a break from the grind of academics, and get some real-world experience. Many colleges even allow students to delay their admission for a year if a gap year is planned. Getting a job is another way to gain life experience and perspective—and can even result in a reverse effect of students hoping to get back to school sooner!*

CONCLUSION:
WILL YOU EMBRACE
YOUR PARENT COMPASS?

The other day, we witnessed something on social media that got us thinking. A mother posted to her Facebook page about how her daughter had been bullied. Apparently a young boy had hurled insults at her daughter behind the thin veil that technology provides these days—insults that are both appalling and too vulgar to repeat here, insults that cut to the core of a young teen as she is coming to realize her identity and mold her self-concept. Understandably, the mom was brokenhearted for her daughter, and she took to social media to plead for advice.

The overwhelming response was what blew us away. Parents supported her in droves, posting scores of empathic comments and suggestions, and all with the equal enthusiasm of a parent whose own child had instead been spurned. Comments continued to pop up over the course of the day, but the one commonality and the thread that wove each of them together: *support*. This hurting-for-her-daughter mom had a community around her, one that came swooping in with empathy as they shared similar stories, kindness as they offered words of encouragement, and sadness as they reflected on the difficult world that our teens must navigate. And as we thought about the message that we wanted to leave with you, our audience, the theme of *community* started to take up the lion's share of that message.

Mold Your Community

During the course of our research for this book, we interviewed researchers from Challenge Success, who walked us through some of the results of their powerful surveys. We were especially intrigued by one in particular. It was a question that asked parents about the qualities that were most important to them when they explored colleges with their children. Only about one third reported that the *US News & World Report* rankings placed among their top three most important criteria. But interestingly, when they were asked to indicate the value that they thought their communities place on the same measure, 64 percent said that rankings were among the top three most important qualities in their communities.[1] Said another way, what we perceive as prevalent in our communities can be much the opposite of the way in which we characterize our own values and priorities. So what are we to do?

Fellow parents, be the change you wish to see. We'll say it again: *be the change you wish to see.* There are so many other parents out there who desire to see some of the very same changes that you do. You've probably had casual conversations about those common complaints in line at the grocery store, during halftime at a football game, or after a PTA meeting. *You have the power to form a community*—to inspire others around you to throw in those orange (or yellow . . . or brightly multicolored!) earplugs—to practice presence, to praise the journey, to facilitate self-advocacy, to encourage downtime. Yes, that's right: you have the power to mold your community and to redirect a path that has gotten alarmingly off track. As the saying goes, start locally and think globally.

Be Brave

But we are not saying that it will be easy. We recognize that the changes we are asking you to make seem big, and they maybe sound scary, but they are possible. You won't get it right all the time, but you'll try, and that's all we're asking. And so the other message with which we want to empower you is this: *be brave.* Be an upstander. Stand UP. Practice those things that you know will lead you to a healthier, more fulfilling life with your child. Prioritize your relationship, your sanity, and your child's sanity over bragging rights at the next cocktail party or in your next Facebook or Instagram post (because, let's be honest, others are just going to roll their eyes anyway). Seek solace in the fact that it is more about what your child does than where your child goes. Equip him to contribute to something valuable with his grit. And know that alongside the courage to change comes the possibility that you might be disliked or—gasp!—"unfriended" or "unfollowed." You might spark debate, you might make other people uncomfortable, you might make them defensive. You might offend. You might even stand out at your child's school to teachers, parents, or administrators who disagree or who want to continue doing things the old way. Yes. But you *also* might become part of a very important movement—a parent compass movement—that is seeking change for a generation of overstressed, over-programmed, and over-exhausted kids.

Remember when we told you that in four years, you, a parent of a thirteen- to seventeen-year-old, can age as much as twenty years? Well, won't that aging be worth it when you can confidently say that you rolled up your sleeves—that you showed up, listened, tuned into your teen, and put in the work to foster grit, resilience, intention, work ethic, kindness, and humility in your future adult—and all of that in the face of the unique challenges that teenagers face today? And maybe you will even be able to say that you inspired other parents—your community—to do the same. You will be able to say with pride, fellow parent, that you truly embraced your parent compass.

ACKNOWLEDGMENTS

They say "it takes a village," and this book certainly did.

From Both Cindy and Jenn

Thank you Familius for believing in the important message of *The Parent Compass* from the very start and for welcoming us so warmly into your family. You are consummate professionals, and we feel privileged to be a part of your community whose mission it is to strive to make families better. To Christopher Robbins for wholeheartedly embracing the need for a book to help parents of adolescents, and to Brooke Jorden and Kate Farrell for your constant patience in answering our barrage of questions. And to our editor Kaylee Mason, whose keen eye and detail-oriented talent made our work shine, and Workman for getting our book distributed.

Thank you to the scores of professionals who believed in our work and advised, supported, and consulted with us along the way including: Dr. Denise Pope of Stanford University and Challenge Success; Than Healy of the Menlo School; Vicky de Felice who introduced us and who patiently consulted and mentored us both through the years; Chelsea Brown and Tiffany Shlain—tech gurus extraordinaire; Dr. Michael Dennin; Kari Riedel and Sarah Miles at Challenge Success; Brian Tickler; and to the too-numerous-to-list teachers, counselors, headmasters, admission directors, and education professionals who interviewed with us and shared your reflections. And to Cynthia Jenkins, PR queen, whose cleverness, talent, and support of our project is beyond compare. We thank you and appreciate all of your efforts. For your time and insights, we are both so grateful.

From Cindy

To my devoted girlfriends who love me no matter what. To Mom and Dad, for your continuous generosity and who model an enduring marriage and friendship spanning sixty-five-plus years. To Mom and Dad Muchnick for always supporting and cheering me on. To Adam, for your unwavering support, love, and partnership; and to my kids Justin, Jacob, Ross, and Alexa whose patience I admire and appreciate as I sat glued to my computer for many months, not always following my parent compass, in order to get these ideas down. And to Sprinkle for dutifully sitting by my side as I wrote and wrote and wrote. I love each of you to the moon and back. And finally, to Jenn: I could not have completed this book without the most perfect, amazing, exceeded-my-expectations-in-every-way partner. From the moment we spoke for ninety minutes by phone in March 12, 2019 (the day Varsity Blues erupted), our professional relationship as colleagues has grown into a trusted partnership and a genuine friendship. I sincerely appreciate everything you have brought to this project, and I could *not* have done this important work without you. Our hearts and souls were both 100 percent in this, and knowing that I had you in my corner gave me the boost I needed to move forward every day. Thank you for sharing this experience with me, one that I know will connect us for the rest of our lives. I adore you and what we have built and are building together (and, I might add, these are the *only* words you have not edited in this entire book!).

From Jenn

Mom and Dad: you taught me that it was cool to love school and indulged my childhood dreams with reams of typewriter paper on which countless iterations of my "debut novel" were written. Thank you for always encouraging me to write. To Kate Conard and Caroline Tickler, for the enthusiastic support from the moment this project became a reality. Thank you for your incomparable editing expertise, for so generously offering me a quiet place to write, and, most of all, for being by my side at every turn—always. Mike and Bev Curtis: Thank you for watching the girls to allow me time to write and for all of your support. To my sweet friends who checked in, cheered me on, and offered invaluable ideas. Mike, my single biggest cheerleader: you push me to be my best self. Thank you for listening, for critiquing half-written chapters, and for . . . well, everything. You are a true partner. Zoe and Corinne, my brown-eyed girls: you make my heart so very full. Thank you for being endlessly patient with me while I chased this dream and for being my constant reminder of the value of a parent compass. And, finally, to Cindy: In short, you inspire me. I have learned so much from you about grit and not taking no for an answer. I love your ability to not take yourself too seriously and admire your humility. We started this journey as colleagues and ended as close friends—a transformation for which I am grateful. Thank you for your constant cheerleading, motivating words of encouragement, and invaluable lessons in motherhood. Your friendship is a gift.

RESOURCES FOR PARENTS

Parent readers, the following pages contain helpful (but by no means exhaustive) resources that may also assist you in your parenting journey. We encourage you to seek out these sources to tune up your own parenting, educational, and wellness interests. Congratulations on your desire for self-improvement and, more importantly, on what you have accomplished so far as a parent. Stay the course. Parenting is certainly a rewarding and exhausting lifelong job. We wish you luck following your parent compass!

Books for Middle and High School Parents

Deresiewicz, William. *Excellent Sheep: The Miseducation of the American Elite and the Way to a Meaningful Life.* Free Press, 2015.

Dukes, Timothy. *The Present Parent Handbook.* Familius, 2017.

Faber, Joanna, and Elaine Mazlish. *How to Talk So Teens Will Listen and Listen So Teens Will Talk.* William Morrow Paperbacks, 2006. (There is a series for every age.)

Gauld, Laura, and Malcolm Gauld. *The Biggest Job We'll Ever Have: The Hyde School Program for Character-Based Education and Parenting.* Scribner, 2003.

Heffernan, Lisa, and Mary Dell Harrington. *Grown and Flown: How to Support Your Teen, Stay Close as a Family, and Raise Independent Adults.* Flatiron Books, 2019.

Kastner, Laura, and Jennifer Wyatt. *Getting to Calm: Cool-Headed Strategies for Parenting Tweens + Teens—Updated and Expanded.* Schuler, 2009.

Lahey, Jessica. *The Gift of Failure.* Harper, 2016.

Lukianoff, Greg, and Jonathan Haidt. *The Coddling of The American Mind: How Good Intentions and Bad Ideas are Setting Up a Generation for Failure.* Penguin, 2018.

Lythcott-Haims, Julie. *How to Raise an Adult: Break Free of the Over-parenting Trap and Prepare Your Kid for Success.* St. Martin's Griffin, 2015.

Mogel, Wendy. *The Blessing of a B Minus: Raising Resilient Teenagers.* Scribner, 2011.

Muchnick, Cynthia. *The Everything Guide to Study Skills.* Adams Media, 2013.

Pope, Denise. *Doing School: How We Are Creating a Generation of Stressed-Out, Materialistic, and Miseducated Students.* Yale University Press, 2003.

Pope, Denise, and Challenge Success. *Overloaded and Underprepared: Strategies for Stronger Schools and Healthy, Successful Kids.* Jossey-Bass/Wiley, 2015.

Riera, Michael. *Uncommon Sense for Parents with Teenagers.* 3rd ed., Ten Speed Press, 2012.

Rinere, Monique. *Countdown to College: The Essential Steps to Your Child's Successful Launch.* Ballantine Books, 2019.

Savage, Marjorie. *You're On Your Own (But I'm Here If You Need Me): Mentoring Your Child during the College Years.* Touchstone, 2009.

Shlain, Tiffany. *24/6: The Power of Unplugging One Day a Week.* Gallery Books, 2019.

Sugarman, Lisa, and Debra Fox Gansenberg. *How to Raise Perfectly Imperfect Kids.* Familius, 2019.

Thacker, Lloyd, editor. *College Unranked: Ending the College Admissions Frenzy.* Harvard University Press, 2005.

Toughs, Paul. *How Children Succeed: Grit, Curiosity, and the Hidden Power of Character.* Houghton Mifflin, 2012.

Wiseman, Rosalind, and Elizabeth Rapoport. *Queen Bee Moms and Kingpin Dads: Dealing with the Parents, Teachers, Coaches, and Counselors Who Can Make—or Break—Your Child's Future.* Crown, 2006.

Books for Parents about Teen Mental Health

Carter, Christine. *The New Adolescence: Raising Happy and Successful Teens in an Age of Anxiety and Distraction.* BenBella Books, 2020.

Damour, Lisa. *Under Pressure: Confronting the Epidemic of Stress and Anxiety in Girls*. Ballantine Books, 2019.

Damour, Lisa. *Untangled: Guiding Teenage Girls through the Seven Transitions into Adulthood*. Ballantine Books, 2017.

Jensen, Frances. *The Teenage Brain: A Neuroscientist's Guide to Raising Adolescent Boys*. Harper, 2016.

Levine, Madeline. *Teach Your Children Well: Why Values and Coping Skills Matter More Than Grades, Trophies or "Fat Envelopes."* HarperCollins, 2012.

Levine, Madeline. *The Price of Privilege: How Parental Pressure and Material Advantage are Creating a Generation of Disconnected and Unhappy Kids*. Harper Perennial, 2008.

Riera, Michael. *Staying Connected to Your Teenager: How to Keep Them Talking to You and How to Hear What They're Really Saying*. Da Capo Press, 2017.

Thompson, Michael. *The Pressured Child: Freeing Our Kids from Performance Overdrive and Helping Them Find Success in School and Life*. Ballantine Books, 2005.

Books for Parenting Beyond the Teen Years

Bruni, Frank. *Where You Go Is Not Who You'll Be: An Antidote to the College Admissions Mania*. Grand Central Publishing, 2016.

Cohen, Harlan. *The Naked Roommate: For Parents Only—A Parent's Guide to the New College Experience*. Sourcebooks, 2012.

Hofer, Barbara K., and Abigail Sullivan Moore. *The Connected Parent: Staying Close to our Kids (and Beyond) While Letting Them Grow Up*. Atria Books, 2011.

Johnson, Helen, and Christine Schelhas-Miller. *Don't Tell Me What to Do, Just Send Money: The Essential Parenting Guide to the College Years*. Golden Guides from St. Martin's Press, Revised ed. 2011.

Levin Coburn, Karen, and Madge Lawrence Treeger. *Letting Go: A Parent's Guide to Understanding the College Years*. 6th ed., William Morrow, 2016.

Pope, Loren. *Colleges That Change Lives*. Penguin Books, 2012.

Tough, Paul. *The Years That Matter Most: How College Makes or Breaks Us*. Houghton Mifflin, 2019.

Books That Brings Families Together

Berger, Brad. *Unplug and Play*. Familius, 2016.

Berger, Warren. *The Beautiful Book of Questions*. Bloomsbury Publishing, 2018.

Greenland, Susan Kaiser and Annika Harris. *Mindful Game Activity Cards: 55 Fun Ways to Share Mindfulness with Kids and Teens*. Shambhala, 2017.

TableTopics. *TableTopics Family: Questions to Start Great Conversations*. Ultra PRO International, LLC, 2011.

The Family Dinner Project. *Eat, Laugh, Talk*. Familius, 2019.

Helpful Parent Websites and Organizations

American Academy of Pediatrics Bright Futures: brightfutures.aap.org.

Bring Change 2 Mind: https://bringchange2mind.org. "A nonprofit organization working together to end the stigma and discrimination surrounding mental illness through widely distributed public education materials and programs based on the latest scientific insights and measured for effectiveness."

Challenge Success: www.challengesuccess.org. "At Challenge Success, we believe that our society has become too focused on grades, test scores, and performance, leaving little time for kids to develop the necessary skills to become resilient, ethical, and motivated learners. We provide families and schools with the practical, research-based tools they need to create a more balanced and academically fulfilling life for kids. After all, success is measured over the course of a lifetime, not at the end of a semester."

Child Mind Institute: "The Child Mind Institute is an independent, national nonprofit dedicated to transforming the lives of children and families struggling with mental health and learning disorders." Also be sure to review the Media and Tech area of that site for more helpful ways to deal with technology in you and your teens' lives.

Colleges That Change Lives: Ctcl.org. "CTCL was founded on a philosophy of building the knowledge, character and values of young people by introducing them to a personalized and transformative collegiate experience. Although the member colleges approach this challenge with varying perspectives, institutional missions, and pedagogical strategies, a student-centered mission is common to all campuses."

Common Sense Media: www.commonsensemedia.org. "Common Sense is dedicated to helping kids thrive in a world of media and technology. We empower parents, teachers, and policymakers by providing unbiased information, trusted advice, and innovative tools to help them harness the power of media and technology as a positive force in all kids' lives." Consult their Family Media Contract for help with tech communication and your teens.

Department of Labor's Office of Apprenticeship: https://www.dol.gov/apprenticeship/ "The go-to website for anyone seeking apprenticeship opportunities as well as helpful links to resources including industry-recognized apprenticeship programs." A "one-stop source for all-things apprenticeship to connect career seekers . . . with apprenticeship resources. Learn more about apprenticeships across industries . . . [and] access open apprenticeship jobs."

DigitalMomTalk.com: Practical, useful, easy-to-implement advice, worksheets, webinars, etc., on all things teen and tech. Curated by Chelsea Brown, Certified Cyber Security Expert and Parent Educator.

Fatherly: www.fatherly.com. "Fatherly is the leading digital media brand for dads. Our mission is to empower men to raise great kids and lead more fulfilling adult lives. From original video series and deep dive reports to podcasts and events, Fatherly offers original reporting, expert parenting advice, and hard-won insights into a challenging, but profoundly rewarding stage of life."

GrownandFlown.com: All-encompassing parenting website with helpful articles on high school, college, a published book, and a newsletter.

HealthyChilren.Org: The American Academy of Pediatrics Website (AAP).

HelpGuide.org: Trusted answers to all questions on mental health and wellness.

Let's Talk Teens: http://lets-talk-teens.org "is a place parents, educators, youth workers, and teens can go to find resources and tools that speak to their circumstances—a place where they can openly share and find a community looking to help teens cope and communicate."

Parentandteen.com: Resource website that aims to strengthen family connections.

Thelearningcommunity.us: A free online parenting resource library that provides tips for parents, parenting videos, and hundreds of links to useful parenting websites with a special area dedicated to teens and tweens.

The Like Movie: thelikemovie.com "A documentary about the impact of social media on our lives." Powerful film experience to share with your teen and their school. Their site has excellent "helpful website" links, too.

Wait Until 8th: www.waituntil8th.org. "The Wait Until 8th pledge empowers parents to rally together to delay giving children a smartphone until at least 8th grade." Consider signing the pledge and joining over 20,000 other parents who support the idea to wait until their children are in eighth grade to own a smartphone.

Gap Year Recommendation Sites

Abroadly.com: One-stop-shop for intern abroad experiences.

Birthright: Taglit-Birthright Israel offers a FREE trip to Israel for Jewish young adults between the ages of eighteen and thirty-two. Birthrighisrael.com.

Global Leadership Adventures: "Explore the world on our summer volunteer programs for high school students abroad. At GLA, we believe meaningful teen travel can be life-changing." Experiencegla.com.

Plan My Gap Year: An award-winning volunteer travel organization, offering life-changing experiences across seventeen countries in Africa, Asia, and South America. www.planmygapyear.com.

Projects-Abroad.org: "The world's largest provider of international volunteering, internships and meaningful travel experiences. Running for over 25 years and trusted by over 120,000 participants who've joined [their] trips."

Study Abroad: IESAbroad.org. Courses and part time internships abroad.

Substance Abuse and Addiction Resources

While *The Parent Compass* does not address drugs and alcohol or technology addiction in the tween and teen years, these are all very serious conditions. Our book could not do those topics justice in great depth, so we are providing resources here. One school counselor notes:

> At the NCADA (National Council on Alcoholism and Drug Abuse) where I've been working for the last ten years, we go into schools daily and present classes on a wide range of topics including character education, resiliency, self-worth, etc. and, of course, the effects of drug and alcohol misuse. We try to help our students take the better path to lead a drug- and alcohol-free life. Sadly, experimentation can begin in the middle school years, which emphasizes the importance of keeping the parents as involved in their child's lives as they were in the elementary years.
>
> —Andy Shanker, St. Louis, MO

If your child is affected by drugs or alcohol, you should start by reaching out to local drug abuse resources in your community or state, especially rehabilitation facilities or hospitals with outpatient programs. These are the professionals who can help parents to manage these crises and provide options for kids and also for the families. Here are a few other places to start:

Facebook.com/partnershipdrugfree/

Substance Abuse and Mental Health Services Administration: https://www.samhsa.gov

National Council on Alcoholism and Drug Abuse (NCADA)

NOTES

Foreword

1. National Academies of Sciences, Engineering, and Medicine. 2019. *Vibrant and Healthy Kids: Aligning Science, Practice, and Policy to Advance Health Equity.* Washington, DC: The National Academies Press. https://doi.org/10.17226/25466.

Introduction

1. "Major Depression." National Institute of Mental Health. Statistics retrieved May 13, 2019, https://www.nimh.nih.gov/health/statistics/major-depression.shtml.

Chapter One

1. Video: https://www.kidsinthehouse.com/teenager/parenting-teens/bonding-with-your-teen/managing-vs-consulting-your-teenager.

2. Than Healy. "Keepers of the Culture," *KnightLine,* Nov 22, 2019.

3. Tim Elmore. "College admissions scandal—Could free range parenting prevent the next disaster?" *Fox News Opinion,* November 23, 2019.

4. "Supportive Relationships and Active Skill-Building Strengthening the Foundations of Resilience: Working Paper 13." *National Scientific Council on the Developing Child* (2015): 2. http://www.developingchild.harvard.edu.

5. Juliana Menasce Horowitz and Nikki Graf. "Most U.S. Teens See Anxiety and Depression as a Major Problem among Their Peers," *Pew Research Center, Social & Demographic Trends,* February 20, 2019.

6. Modified from Liz Evans. "25 Ways to Ask Your Teens 'So How Was School Today?' without Asking Them 'So How Was School Today?'" *The Huffington Post*, December 7, 2017.

7. Gathered from Warren Berger. *The Beautiful Book of Questions*. Bloomsbury Publishing, 2018.

8. Donald Sheff. "Izzy, Did You Ask a Good Question Today?" *The New York Times Opinion*, January 19, 1988, https://www.nytimes.com/1988/01/19/opinion/l-izzy-did-you-ask-a-good-question-today-712388.html.

9. Madeline Levine. *The Price of Privilege*. Harper Perennial, 2006, p. 17.

10. Kirk Carapezza. "The Pressure on Kids—They're Born into It," *WGBH News*, November 18, 2019.

Chapter Two

1. Madeline Levine. "Raising Successful Children." *New York Times Opinion*. Aug 4, 2012. https://www.nytimes.com/2012/08/05/opinion/sunday/raising-successful-children.html.

2. Interview with headmaster, November 23, 2019.

3. Jungmeen Kim-Spoon, Gregory S. Longo, and Michael E. McCullough. "Adolescents who are less religious than their parents are at risk for externalizing and internalizing symptoms: The mediating role of parent-adolescent relationship quality." *Journal of Family Psychology* 26 no. 4 (2012): 636–41.

4. "Supportive Relationships and Active Skill-Building Strengthening the Foundations of Resilience: Working Paper 13." *National Scientific Council on the Developing Child* (2015): 2. http://www.developingchild.harvard.edu.

Chapter Three

1. Carol Dweck. "Dweck Revisits the Growth Mindset." *Education Weekly*, November 13, 2019. https://www.edweek.org/ew/articles/2015/09/23/carol-dweck-revisits-the-growth-mindset.html.

2. R. Weissbourd, S. Jones, T. Ross-Anderson, J. Kahn, and M. Russell. "The children we mean to raise: The real messages adults are sending about values." Making Caring Common Project, Harvard Graduate School of Education (2014). http://sites.gse.harvard.edu/sites/default/files/making-caring-common/files/mcc_the_children_we_mean_to_raise_0.pdf.

3. Carol Dweck. *Mindset: The New Psychology of Success.* Ballantine, 2007.

4. Interview with Michael Dennin, Vice Provost for Teaching and Learning and Dean of the Division of Undergraduate Education, UCI, January 21, 2020.

5. Carol Dweck. "Dweck Revisits the Growth Mindset." *Education Weekly*, November 13, 2019. https://www.edweek.org/ew/articles/2015/09/23/carol-dweck-revisits-the-growth-mindset.html.

6. Carol Dweck. "Dweck Revisits the Growth Mindset." *Education Weekly*, November 13, 2019. https://www.edweek.org/ew/articles/2015/09/23/carol-dweck-revisits-the-growth-mindset.html.

7. Paraphrased from presentation by Lisa Damour. "Under Pressure." Common Ground Speaker Series, Sacred Heart School, December 10, 2019.

8. Than Healy, Menlo School, *KnightTime News*, Fall 2018.

9. Tracy Hargen. "This Is What Happens When You Stop Fixing Things for Your Kids." *Grown and Flown.* Retrieved December 31, 2019. https://grownandflown.com/stop-fixing-things-for-your-kids/.

Chapter Four

1. Daniel J. Siegel and Tina Payne Bryson. "Do you really 'see' your child?" *New York Times.* January 6, 2020. https://parenting. nytimes.com/preschooler/daniel-siegel-tina-payne-bryson.

2. www.scholarshipstats.com/varsityodds.html

3. www.scholarshipstats.com.

4. "Real Sports with Bryant Gumbel 272." *HBO.* November 2019. www.hbo.com/real-sports-with-bryant-gumbel/all-episodes/ november-2019.

5. Baseballbetterment.com.

6. funderstanding.com.

7. https://www.nationalservice.gov/pdf/05_1130_LSA_YHA_ SI_factsheet.pdf.

Chapter Five

1. PDF for Teens, www.challengesuccess.com.

2. "The Sleep Connection." UC Berkeley, Night Owl Study. https://thesleepconnection.com.au/ new-study-kids-whore-night-owls-perform-worse-at-school/.

3. Margie Skeer and E. Ballard. "Are family meals as good for youth as we think they are? A review of the literature on family meals as they pertain to adolescent risk prevention." *Journal of Youth & Adolescence* 42 no. 7 (2013): 943–63.

4. "The importance of family dinners VIII: A CASA Columbia White Paper." National Center on Addiction and Substance Abuse at Columbia University (2012). http://www.casacolumbia.org/addiction-research/reports/ importance-of-family-dinners-2012.

5. The Family Dinner Project. *Eat, Laugh, Talk: The Family Dinner Playbook*. Familius, 2019, p. 16.

6. The Family Dinner Project. *Eat, Laugh, Talk: The Family Dinner Playbook*. Familius, 2019, p. 12.

7. The Family Dinner Project. *Eat, Laugh, Talk: The Family Dinner Playbook*. Familius, 2019.

8. "The importance of family dinners VIII: A CASA Columbia White Paper." National Center on Addiction and Substance Abuse at Columbia University (2012). http://www.casacolumbia.org/addiction-research/reports/importance-of-family-dinners-2012.

9. "Generation M2: Media in the lives of 8- to 18-year-olds." Kaiser Family Foundation (2010): 34. https://www.kff.org/wp-content/uploads/2013/01/8010.pdf.

10. "Challenge Success—Stanford Parent Survey." Challenge Success (2019).

11. Andrea Guthmann. "Tutors, private test prep coaches, homework therapists. Rich kids have all the academic advantages money can buy. But at what cost?" *Chicago Tribune*, April 5, 2019.

12. Marybeth Bock. "It's Easy to Judge until It's Your Kid, Let's Try Compassion." *Grown and Flown*. https://grownandflown.com/stop-judging-other-kids/.

Chapter Six

1. Daniel J. Siegel and Tina Payne Bryson. "Do you really 'see' your child?" *New York Times*. January 6, 2020. https://parenting.nytimes.com/preschooler/daniel-siegel-tina-payne-bryson.

2. Interview with Tiffany Shlain, author of *24/6: The Power of Unplugging One Day a Week*, March 3, 2020.

3. Interview with Chelsea Brown, www.digitalmomtalk.com, January 23, 2020.

4. Centers for Disease Control. "Screen Time vs. Lean Time." Infographic 2018. https://www.cdc.gov/nccdphp/dnpao/multimedia/infographics/getmoving.html.

5. Interview with Tiffany Shlain, author of *24/6: The Power of Unplugging One Day a Week*, March 3, 2020.

6. Nick Bilton. "Steve Jobs Was a Low-Tech Parent," *New York Times*, September 10, 2014.

7. Interview with Chelsea Brown, www.digitalmomtalk.com, January 23, 2020.

8. Interview with Tiffany Shlain, author of *24/6: The Power of Unplugging One Day a Week*, March 3, 2020.

9. Jonathan Haidt and Tobias Rose-Stockwell. "The Dark Psychology of Social Networks: Why It Feels Like Everything Is Going Haywire." *The Atlantic*, December, 2019 (emphasis added).

10. TedxTeen. "ReThink before You Type," Oct 23, 2014. https://www.youtube.com/watch?v=YkzwHuf6C2U and http://www.rethinkwords.com.

11. Chris C. "Love What Matters." Feb. 29, 2020. https://www.lovewhatmatters.com/sick-stomach-cell-phones-social-media-school-principal-parenting/.

12. The Family Dinner Project. *Eat, Laugh, Talk: The Family Dinner Playbook*. Familius, 2019, p. 17.

13. Adrian F. Ward, Kristen Duke, Ayelet Gneezy, Maarten W. Bos. "Brain Drain: The Mere Presence of One's Own Smartphone Reduces Available Cognitive Capacity." *Journal of the Association for Consumer Research* 2, no. 2 (April 2017). https://www.journals.uchicago.edu/doi/abs/10.1086/691462

14. Interview with Tiffany Shlain, author of *24/6: The Power of Unplugging One Day a Week*, March 3, 2020.

15. The Family Dinner Project. *Eat, Laugh, Talk: The Family Dinner Playbook*. Familius, 2019, p. 16.

16. The Family Dinner Project. *Eat, Laugh, Talk: The Family Dinner Playbook*. Familius, 2019, p. 17.

17. Interview with Brian Tickler, January 8, 2019.

18. Hannah Natanson. "Harvard Rescinds Acceptances for at Least Ten Students for Obscene Memes." *The Harvard Crimson*. June 5, 2017. https://www.thecrimson.com/article/2017/6/5/2021-offers-rescinded-memes/.

19. Jeff Schiffman, Director of Admission, Tulane (blog post), January 2020. https://tuadmissionjeff.blogspot.com/2020/01/how-to-stay-admitted.html?m=1&fbclid=IwAR2rdHrE22eWxGoeurvDnHa6pJnQTsbmLuiS0_7OXQU7l0W1tTFO-BNkxmw.

20. Natalie Burg. "At Home Tech Tips to Keep Your Family Connected to Each Other." *Forbes*, February 24, 2020. https://www.forbes.com/sites/capitalone/2020/02/24/at-home-tech-tips-to-keep-your-family-connected-to-each-other/#76ae9a1e25d8.

21. Natalie Burg. "At Home Tech Tips to Keep Your Family Connected to Each Other." *Forbes*, February 24, 2020. https://www.forbes.com/sites/capitalone/2020/02/24/at-home-tech-tips-to-keep-your-family-connected-to-each-other/#76ae9a1e25d8.

22. Interview with Chelsea Brown, www.digitalmomtalk.com, January 23, 2020.

Chapter Eight

1. Interview with teacher, January 1, 2020.

2. Paraphrased from presentation by Lisa Damour. "Under Pressure" presentation, Common Ground Speaker Series, Sacred Heart School, December 20, 2020.

3. Paraphrased from presentation by Lisa Damour. "Under Pressure" presentation, Common Ground Speaker Series, Sacred Heart School, December 20, 2020.

4. www.challengesuccess.com. http://www.challengesuccess.org/wp-content/uploads/2018/10/CS_Flyer_Teens_042018_5.pdf.

5. Interview with Michael Dennin, Vice Provost for Teaching and Learning and Dean of the Division of Undergraduate Education, UCI, January 21, 2020.

6. Interview with headmaster, November 23, 2019.

7. Interview with teacher, January 8, 2020.

8. Interview with teacher, January 11, 2020.

9. Interview with headmaster, November 23, 2019.

Chapter Nine

1. Valerie Strauss. "*US News* Changed the Way It Ranks Colleges. It's Still Ridiculous." *The Washington Post*, September 12, 2018. https://www.washingtonpost.com/education/2018/09/12/us-news-changed-way-it-ranks-colleges-its-still-ridiculous/.

2. Valerie Strauss. "*US News* Changed the Way It Ranks Colleges. It's Still Ridiculous." *The Washington Post*, September 12, 2018. https://www.washingtonpost.com/education/2018/09/12/us-news-changed-way-it-ranks-colleges-its-still-ridiculous/.

3. Lynn O'Shaughnessy. "Can College Rankings Giant Keep Schools from Cheating?" *The College Solution* 2013. http://www.thecollegesolution.com/can-college-rankings-giant-keep-school s-from-cheating/.

4. Max Kutner. "How to Game the College Rankings." *Boston Magazine,* August 26, 2014. https://www.bostonmagazine.com/news/2014/08/26/how-northeastern-gamed-the-college-rankings/2/.

5. Douglas Belkin. "For Sale: SAT-Takers' Names. Colleges Buy Student Data and Boost Exclusivity." *The Wall Street Journal.* https://www.wsj.com/articles/for-sale-sat-takers-names-college s-buy-student-data-and-boost-exclusivity-11572976621_.

6. Valerie Strauss. "*US News* Changed the Way It Ranks Colleges. It's Still Ridiculous." *The Washington Post,* September 12, 2018. https://www.washingtonpost.com/education/2018/09/12/us-news-changed-way-it-ranks-colleges-its-still-ridiculous/.

7. Liberal Arts Colleges. "14 Reasons Why *US News* College Rankings Are Meaningless." https://www.liberalartscolleges.com/us-news-college-rankings-meaningless/.

8. Malcolm Gladwell. "The Trouble with College Rankings: What College Rankings Really Tell Us." *New Yorker,* February 6, 2011. https://www.newyorker.com/magazine/2011/02/14/the-order-of-things.

9. Ted O'Neill. "Admissions failure." Speech delivered at Weissbourd Conference, May 2016. https://thepointmag.com/examined-life/admissions-failure/.

10. Interview with headmaster, November 23, 2019.

11. "A 'Fit' Over Rankings: Why College Engagement Matters More Than Selectivity [White Paper]." Challenge Success (October, 2018). https://www.challengesuccess.org/resources/research/white-papers/.

12. Interview with Michael Dennin, Vice Provost for Teaching and Learning and Dean of the Division of Undergraduate Education, UCI, January 21, 2020.

13. Alexandra Rhodes, Rhodes Educational Consulting, Facebook, December 18, 2019.

14. Lisa Micele, University of Illinois Laboratory School Urbana, IL, Facebook, April 30, 2019.

Chapter Ten

1. Jennifer Levitz and Melissa Korn. "'Why Didn't You Believe in Me?' The Family Reckoning after the College Admissions Scandal." *Wall Street Journal*, January 17, 2020.

2. Jennifer Levitz and Melissa Korn. "'Why Didn't You Believe in Me?' The Family Reckoning after the College Admissions Scandal." *Wall Street Journal*, January 17, 2020.

3. Jennifer Levitz and Melissa Korn. "'Why Didn't You Believe in Me?' The Family Reckoning after the College Admissions Scandal." *Wall Street Journal*, January 17, 2020.

4. John Woolfolk. "College Scandal: This Bay Area student newspaper nixed a popular map of where seniors are bound for college." *The Mercury News*, May 28, 2019. https://www.mercurynews.com/2019/05/24/college-scandal-this-bay-area-student-newspaper-nixed-a-popular-map-of-where-seniors-are-bound-for-college/.

5. Anonymous parent, Facebook (on *Writing Successful College Applications* Facebook page), May 29, 2019.

Chapter Eleven

1. Courtney E. Ackerman. "Cognitive Distortions: When your brain lies to you." *Positive Psychology*, 2019. https://positivepsychology.com/cognitive-distortions/.

Chapter Twelve

1. Mike Rowe, Facebook, February 17, 2015.

2. Content in this section adapted from Justin Muchnick. *Teens' Guide to College & Career Planning*, Peterson's Publishers, 2016.

3. Mike Colagrassi. "Why the College Dropout Myth Can Hurt Your Prospects," *Big Think*, October 23, 2018. https://bigthink.com/personal-growth/college-dropout-myth-can-hurt-career.

Conclusion

1. "Challenge Success—Stanford Parent Survey." *Challenge Success* 2019.

INDEX

Educational Consultant 1; 86; 87; 111

Empathy 93; 130; 131; 132; 153; 163; 165; 181

Extracurricular Activities i; 10; 11; 24; 49; 51; 52; 53; 73; 81; 82; 151; 154

F

Failure 11; 20; 38; 41; 42; 81; 111; 117; 120; 122; 123; 127; 137; 142; 155; 156; 159; 163; 189; 190; 207

Family Dinner 23; 76; 77; 102; 192; 202; 203; 204; 205

Family Meals 75; 77; 101; 202

Family Media Agreement 94

Family Time 71; 72; 124; 195

Flip Phone 97

Focusing on the Negative 161; 162

G

Games 24; 26; 29; 30; 35; 55; 57; 58; 61; 62; 65; 66; 67; 69; 72; 76; 78; 79; 106; 107; 136; 147; 160; 163; 165; 169; 182; 195

Gap Year 170; 171; 172; 173; 179; 195; 196

Gates, Bill 178

Gladwell, Malcolm 54; 137; 207

Goal Setting 49; 109; 110; 111; 113; 115; 117; 118

GPA 36; 37; 119

Gratitude 125; 127; 128; 162

Grit 9; 35; 38; 41; 120; 130; 160; 183; 187; 190; 218

Growth Mindset 35; 36; 38; 41; 43; 200; 201

H

Hearing versus Listening 16; 17; 18; 19; 47; 73; 81; 89; 102; 151; 187

O

Operation Varsity Blues 1; 153; 154; 186

P

Parent Behavior toward Teachers 127

Parent Partner 128; 129

Playtime 72; 124

Playtime, Downtime, and Family Time 72; 124

Pope, Denise ii; 2; 13; 185

Presence 17; 92; 93; 96; 101; 102; 133; 137; 182; 204

R

Rankings 9; 13; 133; 134; 135; 136; 137; 138; 139; 182; 206; 207

Rejection 29; 157

Resilience 9; 12; 30; 38; 41; 42; 56; 120; 130; 157; 160; 183; 199; 200

ReThink 99; 204

S

SAT 135; 152; 166; 206

School Is a Job 13; 119; 120

Screen Time 98; 102

Self-advocate ii; 9; 10; 12; 33; 43; 45; 56; 85; 126; 137

Shlain, Tiffany 3; 94; 185; 203; 204

Siegel, Daniel J. 48; 92; 201; 203

Sleep i; 14; 18; 52; 73; 74; 75; 96; 100; 202

Snowplow Parent 10; 43

Social Media 7; 65; 74; 75; 89; 92; 93; 96; 97; 98; 99; 100; 103; 104; 105; 157; 160; 181; 194; 195

ABOUT THE CO-AUTHORS

About Cynthia Clumeck Muchnick, MA

Cindy, a graduate of Stanford University, is an expert in the college admission process: she got her start in admission offices before opening a private study skills and college counseling business in Southern California, which she ran for over fifteen years. As an Assistant Director of Admission for the Illinois Institute of Technology and the University of Chicago, she screened and reviewed over three thousand applications, interviewed prospective students, and served on the admission committee to evaluate borderline applicants and appeals cases. Then, as a private counselor, she helped hundreds of high school students navigate their academic journeys, including course selection, study skills, time management, and college applications. Since closing her private educational practice in 2011, Cindy has focused on public speaking to student, parent, school, and business groups on a variety of education-related topics.

Over the course of her career, Cindy has written numerous books: *The Parent Compass* is her tenth. Her other titles include *The Best College Admission Essays* (co-author, ARCO/Peterson's, 1997), *The Everything Guide to Study Skills: Strategies, Tips, and Tools You Need to Succeed in School* (F&W Media, 2011), *Straight-A Study Skills* (co-author, Adams Media, 2012), *The Everything College Checklist Book* (F&W Media, 2013), *Writing Successful College Applications: It's More Than Just the Essay* (Peterson's Publishing, 2014), and four other books (Simon & Schuster and Random House).

Cindy holds a bachelor's degree in Political Science and Art History from Stanford University and a master's degree in Liberal Studies from Nova Southeastern University. Some of the other twists and turns in her multifaceted career include her stints as a campus tour guide and volunteer student coordinator for Stanford's Office of Undergraduate Admission, and a tenth-grade history teacher at The University School, in Ft. Lauderdale, Florida.

Cindy raised her family in Newport Beach, CA, and moved to Menlo Park, CA, in 2018, where she resides with her husband and four children. For further information, or to inquire about a potential speaking engagement, feel free to visit her website at www.cynthiamuchnick.com.

About Jenn Curtis, MSW

Jenn Curtis owns FutureWise Consulting, an educational consulting company in Orange County, California. She has guided hundreds of high school students from throughout the United States through all aspects of the college admission process. Her passion lies in empowering students to navigate their high school years with confidence, emphasizing self-advocacy, grit, and intention.

Jenn's interest in mental health and research began while an undergraduate at the University of California–Los Angeles (UCLA), where she worked in a lab studying athletic performance anxiety. After college, at the University of California–Irvine's Child Development Center, Jenn researched treatments for learning disabilities, co-authored a published study on a novel diagnostic tool for ADHD, and supervised and trained undergraduate researchers. After earning her master's degree, Jenn worked in psychiatric rehabilitation, assisting clients with severe and persistent mental illness. She also served as the Director of Grant Writing for an international university, was an editorial assistant for a forensic psychology academic journal, has edited several books, and coached graduate and doctoral students in developing effective writing skills. Jenn also developed a college and career readiness program for first-generation students.

Jenn earned her bachelor's degree in psychology from UCLA's Honors College and master's degree in social work from the University of Southern California, where she was elected to the Phi Kappa Phi Honor Society and selected as Dean's Scholar. Jenn earned her College Counseling Certificate from UCLA. She resides in San Clemente, California, with her husband and two daughters. For more information on FutureWise Consulting or to inquire about speaking engagements, visit www.futurewiseconsulting.com.

You can also visit www.parentcompassbook.com for current information, events, and author appearances related to *The Parent Compass*.

ABOUT FAMILIUS

Visit Our Website: www.familius.com

Familius is a global trade publishing company that publishes books and other content to help families be happy. We believe that the family is the fundamental unit of society and that happy families are the foundation of a happy life. We recognize that every family looks different, and we passionately believe in helping all families find greater joy. To that end, we publish books for children and adults that invite families to live the Familius Nine Habits of Happy Family Life: *love together, play together, learn together, work together, talk together, heal together, read together, eat together,* and *laugh together.* Founded in 2012, Familius is located in Sanger, California.

Connect

Facebook: www.facebook.com/paterfamilius
Twitter: @familiustalk, @paterfamilius1
Pinterest: www.pinterest.com/familius
Instagram: @familiustalk

FAMILIUS

The most important work you ever do will be within the walls of your own home.

For more information on *The Parent Compass* please follow, visit, and subscribe to:
Twitter: @ParentCompass1
Instagram: @parentcompass
Facebook: TheParentCompass
parentcompassbook@gmail.com
www.parentcompassbook.com